PLAY TODAY
Building the Young Brain through Creative Expression

Ann Barbour, PhD

PLAY TODAY
Building the Young Brain
through Creative Expression

Ann Barbour, PhD

Gryphon House
www.gryphonhouse.com

Published by Gryphon House, Inc.
P. O. Box 10, Lewisville, NC 27023
800.638.0928; 877.638.7576 (fax)
Visit us on the web at www.gryphonhouse.com.

Library of Congress Cataloging-in-Publication Data
Names: Barbour, Ann, author.
Title: Play today : building the young brain through creative expression / by
  Ann Barbour, PhD.
Description: Lewisville, NC : Gryphon House, Inc., 2016. | Includes
  bibliographical references and index.
Identifiers: LCCN 2015036470 | ISBN 9780876596616
Subjects: LCSH: Play. | Creative ability in children. | Early childhood
  education.
Classification: LCC LB1140.35.P55 B37 2016 | DDC 372.21--dc23 LC record available
at http://lccn.loc.gov/2015036470

Bulk Purchase
Gryphon House books are available for special premiums and sales promotions as well as for fund-raising use. Special editions or book excerpts also can be created to specifications. For details, call 800.638.0928.

Disclaimer
Gryphon House, Inc., cannot be held responsible for damage, mishap, or injury incurred during the use of or because of activities in this book. Appropriate and reasonable caution and adult supervision of children involved in activities and corresponding to the age and capability of each child involved are recommended at all times. Do not leave children unattended at any time. Observe safety and caution at all times.

PREFACE

My fascination with dramatic play began as I witnessed my own sons' rich fantasy play. I realized no amount of forethought or planning on my part could have engaged them more. What interested and concerned them as young children, and how they were making sense of their experiences, was visible through the scenarios they enacted. Over the years, I also observed hundreds of young children in my classroom eagerly initiating and joining in pretend play and other forms of creative expression. I learned more about each of them in the process. I saw their social competence, language, and cognition blossom through these self-initiated and self-structured activities. I recognized their needs and challenges more fully. I also realized the extent to which dramatic play and creative activities integrate learning and can be central to curriculum.

My graduate studies and subsequent twenty-some years of teaching under-graduate and graduate courses in play helped me further grasp its fundamental role in children's healthy development and learning. I hold in high esteem all those whose research and practice contributes to the professional knowledge base and helps me continue to deepen my understanding. Just like children, we in early childhood are accustomed to learning from each other! I hope this book will aid your own understanding and will help you nurture children's dramatic play and creativity.

To that end, this book is dedicated to all early childhood educators whose passion for encouraging children's optimal development and learning translates into hundreds of daily decisions and interactions. It is also for my sons, Evan and Nathan, whose innovative enterprises continue to amaze me, and for Alan, whose curiosity, intellectual integrity, and constant support sustain me.

TABLE OF CONTENTS

CHAPTER

1

Dramatic Play and Creative Expression in Children's Lives

More and more, people recognize what experts in child development and innovators in early education have known all along: play is foundational to children's development and learning. In fact, the first preschool and kindergarten programs were based on learning through play—activities children choose and carry out by themselves. Friedrich Froebel, the father of the kindergarten; Maria Montessori, whose educational methods are used throughout the world; Jean Piaget, the great developmental psychologist; and Loris Malaguzzi, founder of the Reggio Emilia approach, emphasized the importance of providing environments that motivate children to actively engage in their own endeavors, ones in which they are not directly told what to do or how to do it. The work of these pioneers in early learning has inspired countless child-centered programs. Perhaps they have influenced the approaches you use in your own work.

> **Play is foundational to children's development and learning.**

In recent years, there has been considerable interest in the importance of play. Early childhood professional organizations advocate for it. Journalists write about it in the popular press. Research abounds on how play shapes children's brains and optimizes learning. A 2007 article by researcher Kenneth Ginsburg, "The Importance of Play in Promoting Healthy Child Development and Maintaining Strong Parent-Child Bonds," links free and unstructured play with healthy development. Corporations such as IBM promote its application to innovation and future success. Commercial enterprises provide play spaces and play-based programs for children. Local governments invest public funds to build community playgrounds. A proliferation of Internet blogs, websites, and videos describe how play—particularly imaginative or pretend play—facilitates learning and development.

So what is this activity that is as natural for young children as sleeping and eating? Why has play inspired such renewed interest? Child development and early education experts struggle to define play concisely; yet, there is general agreement on its characteristics.

- Play is freely chosen, actively engaging, intrinsically motivating, and fun.

- Play is process oriented, that is, carried on for its own sake rather than to accomplish some specific goal.

- Play is nonliteral. In play, children distort reality in some fashion. We call the nonliteral nature of play fantasy, pretend, make-believe, or dramatic. Children create their own realities by letting an object or action symbolize something that in reality it is not. They use blocks as phones, build castles out of sand, strum imaginary guitars, and put on capes to rescue playmates from the bad guys.

Unlike adults, children don't struggle to define play. They will show you or tell you that play is what they want to do rather than what they have to do. They have an innate need to explore and act on their environment as they attempt to make sense of it. It is through their own endeavors that children learn about the world, how it functions, what their place is in it, and what effect their own actions have on it. Trying to understand these basic things is common to people of all ages. It's just that adults usually go about figuring things out through other avenues. On the whole, adults are less curious, less flexible in their thinking, less imaginative, and less willing to take risks than young children are. Children's need to know is evident in the hundreds of questions they ask every day. Less obvious to us are the internal processes through which they create meaning. They continually synthesize information from new experiences by making connections to what they already know, thus constructing their own understandings and hypotheses of the world in which they live. When they have a problem or are puzzled by something—say, reaching the bananas on the counter or wondering why there are ants in the kitchen—they rely on these connections. They might use an available item to make a stool, an ingenious solution. Or they might imagine the cat chased the ants inside, an improbable cause. Their actions and speculations demonstrate flexible thinking and, often, indifference to other peoples' opinions.

Perhaps these descriptions remind you of children you know or memories of your own childhood. I remember watching a three-year-old from my kitchen window after a summer downpour. Across the street a big mud puddle had formed near the sidewalk, something novel in our neighborhood. He tapped his foot into the puddle several times, feeling its consistency. He carefully stepped into the muck and stood very quietly for a moment. And then he began to jump and splash with great excitement. The flying mud delighted him. Bending over, he squeezed it in his fists. Next, he sat down, kicked his feet back and forth and then lay on his back to try to make the equivalent of snow angels in the mud. He was obviously enthralled by this new experience, by how the mud looked, felt, and responded to his actions. I don't think his parents shared my amused reaction and probably not my approval when he came in the back door. But I hoped they accepted and perhaps even understood why he was compelled to play in the mud and what he gained from that experience (besides a need for a bath). Not only was this child investigating the properties of mud and seeing what he could do with and in it, he was reveling in expressing himself.

PLAY TODAY

A generation or two ago, children were more often engaged in spontaneously playful activities of this kind. More young children were cared for in their own homes, and there were times during the day when most children were left to their own devices. Parents, particularly mothers, were busy with household tasks or caring for younger children and were happy to have older children occupy themselves. Regardless of the family's economic circumstances or cultural background, most homes had a few toys and a good variety of everyday items or "loose parts." Children used the materials on hand to create worlds from their imaginations. They lined up chairs to make cars they could drive. They dressed in articles of clothing and stepped into the roles these clothes represented. They clomped around in their parents' shoes as they prepared for work or a trip to the store. They cooked imaginary birthday cakes and blew out the candles, and they created shoe-box homes for their dolls. There were usually other children around to introduce novelty. They planned what they would do by telling other children, "Let's pretend . . .," and then decided who would be and do what. They organized games in their neighborhoods. Even though parents were busy, they were usually available to watch, to answer questions, or to settle conflicts that arose. What occurred happened naturally. It was taken for granted as part of the fabric of family life. Parents were grateful that children could entertain themselves, but they were less conscious of all the things children were learning in the process.

For the great majority of children today, these times are gone. Children are playing less. Their everyday experiences are influenced by changes in family structures and roles, economic circumstances, neighborhood environments, educational policies and standards, commercial interests, and the infusion of technology into every aspect of our lives. The proliferation of screen technology and the amount of time children spend watching television and videos and using mobile devices has increased dramatically in recent years. According to a recent research summary by the Campaign for a Commercial-Free Childhood, estimates for the time preschool children spend with screen media range from 2.2 to 4.6 hours a day. While many questions remain about the effects of screen technology on children's minds and bodies, there are growing concerns about what children are not experiencing and doing in this era of digital childhood.

Many schools have reduced recess or have eliminated it altogether in an effort to provide more time for "on task" work and to increase the school's academic ranking. Parents schedule structured activities for their children with the understandable goals of promoting their achievement, cultivating their talents, keeping them safe, and occupying them in constructive activities. Many children are fortunate to have these kinds of opportunities. Nonetheless, over-scheduling diminishes opportunities for hands-on creative play. The combined effects of these social changes means that the contexts in which children grow up today are very different than they were in their parents' and certainly their grandparents' generations. Their opportunities for play—self-chosen and self-structured activities—have diminished.

Even though the circumstances influencing childhood are rapidly changing, the underlying processes through which children develop and learn have not changed. They still literally and figuratively crawl before they walk and walk before they run. They still learn to communicate through trial and error and the responses and examples of those who care for them. They still construct their understandings of the world around them and their place in it through firsthand experiences interacting with objects and people. And there are still important life skills that children need to build to be successful in school and beyond. Play in general helps build many of these fundamental skills. Dramatic play in particular is closely associated with children's learning.

DRAMATIC PLAY AND CREATIVE EXPRESSION

In addition to exploratory play like that of the child splashing in the mud, children's "sense-making" hinges on how they actively process and reprocess their firsthand experiences to understand them better. The main way young children do this is through dramatic play. They are adept at re-creating the life experiences that are most meaningful to them. Dramatic play enables them to control the scale and complexity of these experiences to better grasp their meaning. Unlike exploration or imitation, in dramatic play children create something new and different from external reality. Toddlers and two-year-olds may begin by imitating others as they practice simple actions, but they transi-

tion quickly from this kind of practice play. Preschoolers are not merely imitating the behaviors of a parent when they play house, although their parents' actions inform their play. Instead, dramatic play enables them to determine what it means to be a parent in relation to what they already know. It's common to see children reconstruct some aspects of their experiences over and over again with different variations. This is because as their understandings grow, their play changes and becomes more complex.

Dramatic play is also a form of self-expression. When children pretend, they are representing what they know about things that interest and concern them, however incomplete their knowledge may appear to adults. This form of self-expression aids understanding in the same way that many adults find that talking or writing clarifies their thinking. Young children are able to express through dramatic play what they do not yet have the verbal skills to communicate. Pretending provides a safe and nonjudgmental context for exercising a variety of intellectual skills.

Other ways that children make sense of their experiences and express their understandings are through what teachers who are inspired by the Reggio Emilia approach to early education think of as children's natural "languages." These modes of expression include drawing, painting, sculpture, collage, music, and movement. They too involve symbolic thinking, just as conventional language and dramatic play do. After all, a word such as *car*, whether spoken or written, is a symbol; it stands for the actual thing. The gestures and objects children use to pretend to drive a car symbolize what they know about cars and how to operate them. Likewise, drawing a picture of a car or of their parents, siblings, and themselves depicts their knowledge of cars and their family. These kinds of symbolic representations help children cement their understandings.

Dramatic play and creativity go hand in hand. Both rely on children's symbolic thinking. Both involve drawing on experiences to make connections, imagine possibilities, and deal with ambiguity or, in other words, to hold contradictory or opposing ideas. For example, children realize that a good idea that solves one problem can simultaneously create other problems, and that realization helps them develop reasoning skills and deal with conflict. In dramatic play and other creative activities, children use both *divergent* and *convergent thinking*. Initially, they imagine many ways to play out a particular scenario or express themselves creatively. This is called divergent thinking. After weighing possibilities, they switch to convergent thinking to carry out the one way they have settled on. They shift back and forth between these two forms of thinking at appropriate times in the creative process.

You may recall similar examples of children's symbolic representations from observing your own children or the children you teach. I am reminded of a three-year-old who danced around the playground pretending she was a fairy godmother with a magic wand who could transform other children and playground equipment into characters of her own imagination. I also remember the group of four-year-old "kittens" who minded their five-year-old "mother cat" friend whose pet cat had just had a litter, and the six-year-olds who built a fort out of packing crates and newly trimmed branches from which they made forays to capture prisoners. I also think of the three-year-old who painted an entire sheet of easel paper yellow after a trip to the fire station because "everything there was yellow," and my own son who sculpted hairy mango pits to resemble the features of each person in our family.

What do all these activities have in common? Why are children compelled to play out scenarios and invent environments and objects from their own imaginings? It is unlikely adults would plan these particular activities for children. Yet, given unstructured time, space, and materials, children spontaneously experiment, envision, plan, and carry out situations and create objects of their own design—

ones that are most meaningful to them at the time. In the process, they build foundational skills and concepts, and they delight in self-expression. They feel a sense of accomplishment and joy because they are in control of their actions.

DRAMATIC PLAY AT DIFFERENT STAGES

The early stages of play involve exploration and practice. Infants crawl to investigate the measuring cups in a bottom kitchen drawer. Toddlers and two-year-olds repeatedly nest or stack those cups, but they may also pretend to drink out of them. This emergence of symbolic play in the second year of life (between twelve and twenty-four months) is an indication of children's developing cognitive abilities to make objects, gestures, actions, and, eventually, words stand for or represent something or someone else. As children grow, the gestures, actions, and language that accompany their representations and creative expressions become more complex. Pretend play that is initially centered on themselves starts to involve others. Toddlers who pretended to drink from a cup soon give their stuffed animals a drink. Three-year-olds depend less on realistic objects such as a real cup to prompt dramatic play. They may substitute another object, such as a clam shell, for a cup. Later, they are able to rely on just the mental image of a cup. Simple actions are organized into sequences and pretend scenarios, such as making tea and having a tea party. This progression in children's ability to represent their experiences parallels the development of language and literacy from concrete to more abstract.

The preschool years have been called the golden age of symbolic play. Whereas younger children's play is mainly solitary or parallel (when they play next to another child), the play of preschool and kindergarten children becomes increasingly social. Aptly termed *socio-dramatic play*, it is the primary form of play for four- to six-year-olds. It is person oriented rather than object oriented, and be-

cause of that, it is considered to be a higher level of symbolic play behavior. In addition to transforming objects and actions symbolically, socio-dramatic play entails role-play, where children transform themselves, pretending to be someone or something they are not. The gestures, actions, language, and objects they use must be consistent with the roles they assume. They also must coordinate their roles with those of other children. Doing so requires communicating outside the play to negotiate roles, plan actions, and solve conflicts: "I am the mommy and you are the baby, and I'm going to fix you something to eat." Then it requires ongoing communication within the play itself: "Here's some nice warm soup." As their play evolves, children move back and forth between reality—"Let's pretend I have to get ready for work,"—and fantasy—"Bye-bye, honey. I'll be home soon." This transition in and out of the play frame helps children communicate and understand social cues. They learn to interpret the behaviors of other children and respond appropriately. This process also helps them understand that other people's thoughts and feelings can be different from their own.

Pretend play with others provides multidimensional opportunities for learning and practicing skills in all areas of development as children create complex scenarios together. Play usually lasts for at least ten minutes, but it can be much longer as play partners coordinate roles, communicate, and interact to enact pretend episodes.

Preschool and kindergarten children also create the physical frameworks for their play. Sometimes their efforts focus mainly on constructing things together such as roads and tunnels in the sand. At other times, their creations become stages for dramatic play. They might assemble everyday materials to set up a hospital or shoe store, and then take the roles of doctors and patients, shoe sellers and customers. In either case, the structures or settings they create represent what they understand about such things. Simultaneously, the process of creating these frameworks themselves enables children to acquire and refine fundamental skills.

INDIVIDUAL DIFFERENCES IN DRAMATIC PLAY

Many factors influence children's dramatic play. You may have noticed differences in the amount, themes, roles, degree of realism, use of language, and level of activity in their pretend play. As described earlier, age is a primary factor. Toddlers and two- and three-year-olds often engage in solitary dramatic play, and their play is usually object oriented. They may pretend to drive a car or put a stuffed animal to bed. They also can be directors, making their toys act out particular sequences of actions, as can older children who are playing alone. In group situations, three- to six-year olds usually join together in person-oriented fantasy play. The roles they choose can be more or less realistic. In general, younger children in this age range tend to act out realistic themes based on everyday experiences—say, pretending to be a mommy or brother—and they are more reliant on realistic props to stimulate their play. As children's experiences in the world increase and their symbolic abilities develop, they are more likely to enact roles that are less family centered, less realistic, and less dependent on realistic props.

Gender can also influence themes and roles. Girls more often adopt domestic and person-based themes and roles; whereas, boys tend to gravitate toward adventure and object-based themes and roles. It's quite common to see a girl pretending to be a mother or a particular storybook character and to see a boy driving a car or becoming a superhero. As in other areas, boys tend to be more physically active and less verbal in their fantasy play. Boys also tend to have more gender-typed interests than girls do. For example, they might be less inclined to play house than girls would be to put out a pretend fire. Since play is based on daily experiences, exposure to screen media also influences the content of children's play. More exposure results in less realistic themes and roles.

Socioeconomic status may also be a variable in the amount and depth of children's socio-dramatic play. It should be noted, however, that research finds varying effects of class and economics. Any actual differences might be attributed to access to play materials and environments that support play as well as experiences that inspire it. Culture, parenting styles, and family expectations may also affect children's dramatic play.

It is important to remember that these are tendencies, meaning that on average more or fewer children of a particular age, gender, or background will display these differences. Tendencies should not be interpreted as expectations for how individual children will or should play. Nonetheless, knowing there may be differences in dramatic play can help you plan accordingly and maximize the opportunities children have.

DRAMATIC PLAY AND INNOVATION

More than two thousand years ago, the Greek philosopher Heraclitus said, "Change is the only constant." We could argue that change has sped up considerably since his time. None of us can know what children's lives will be like in five years, let alone in twenty years. Babies born today may live to see the twenty-second century. We can only guess what political, social, economic, or technological developments will transform their daily lives. Adapting to and thriving in rapidly changing times requires more than basic academic skills. It demands resourcefulness, flexibility, teamwork, a creative frame of mind, and an internal sense of responsibility and self-discipline. It also requires a willingness to take risks—to generate and test new ideas without fear of failing or being discouraged by the preconceptions or evaluations of others.

In the current intense focus on common standards to ensure children measure up on standardized tests, opportunities for learning these kinds of skills and attitudes are often lost. In his 2006 *TED Talk*, "Do Schools Kill Creativity?" noted innovation and creativity expert Sir Ken Robinson said, "We don't grow into creativity. We grow out of it. Or rather, we get educated out of it." A 2010 *Newsweek* article by Po Bronson and Ashley Merryman, "The Creativity Crisis," quotes faculty of a major Chinese university on the topic of America's focus on standardized curriculum, "You're racing toward our old model. But we're racing toward your model, as fast as we can." That same year, 1,500 IBM executives from around the world who were surveyed selected creativity as the most important factor for future success. If our only focus is on helping children meet challenges in the world as we now know it, we may not be preparing them for what lies ahead.

If our only focus is on helping children meet challenges in the world as we now know it, we may not be preparing them for what lies ahead.

Creativity is not solely connected to the arts. It involves using previous experiences to create new connections to solve problems. Every field emphasizes thinking outside the box. In elementary and high school classrooms, an emphasis on project-based learning has been shown to increase students' problem-solving abilities and creativity. And indeed, projects conducted with younger children that enable them to investigate and display answers to their own questions provide many opportunities to develop these intellectual dispositions and skills. Be that as it may, dramatic play, the primary form of play for preschool and kindergarten children, is associated with high levels of creativity.

Dramatic play provides a risk-free arena where children can explore and experiment with ideas, test and evaluate their skills, and add to and change the environment in their own ways. In role-play, children act as if they are someone else, imagining and weighing possibilities. This helps them analyze situations from different perspectives. Pretending to be someone else, with all the gestures, actions, and language that entails, also gives children practice thinking divergently as they consider different things they can pretend to do. After they have decided what and how to play, their attention shifts to staging the play they have planned. Their thinking becomes more convergent. Creativity and innovation rely heavily on divergent thinking, but to accomplish goals, convergent thinking is also necessary. It's no wonder that research shows that young children who spend a good deal of time role-playing have high scores on measures of creativity.

If you are like most teachers, you hope the children you teach will be lifelong learners. Even though that term is somewhat cliché, its connection to personal growth and social progress cannot be overstated. Lifelong learning requires a desire to figure things out, to actively make sense by making personal connections, to look at things from different perspectives and imagine possibilities, and to be unafraid of making mistakes. Do these attitudes and skills remind you of the things young children do in creative play?

CHAPTER

2

Learning through Dramatic Play and Other Creative Activities

Have you ever been questioned by colleagues or parents about the benefits of dramatic play or the other creative arts? If so, some of the following might help fuel your responses.

Even though it is customary to describe learning in different developmental domains, creative play integrates learning across these areas because it engages the whole child. It also provides optimal conditions for healthy brain development. For example, in dramatic play, children use abstract or symbolic thinking and language. They refine their conceptual understandings and problem-solving capabilities. They develop social, emotional, and physical competencies. Acting out roles, drawing, painting and constructing art pieces, or creating or moving to music can be thought of as whole-brain activities because they engage many parts of the brain simultaneously.

BRAIN DEVELOPMENT

Neuroscience shows that play stimulates brain development, which is more rapid and extensive in the early years than previously realized. In play children integrate brain functions. During their first thirty-six months, children make approximately one quadrillion synaptic connections in their brains. Synapses are the structures that pass information in the form of electrical or chemical signals from one cell to another to create neural pathways. These pathways enable us to process information, or in other words, to think. Children's interactions, explorations, and play in a world where everything is new result in these myriad connections. It is no wonder that by the time they are three years old, their brains are two-and-a-half times more active than those of adults, and they have far more synaptic connections. This proliferation of connections prepares them to adapt to any type of physical and cultural environment. But since children don't grow up in limitless environments, after about the age of three the connections they use are strengthened while those that are not used disappear. This process of synaptic pruning results in a neural system best suited to the environment in which each child grows and learns.

Play of all sorts facilitates brain development, first by helping to create those synaptic connections and later by strengthening the connections that will be most useful.

Brain development can be adversely affected when children are stressed, understimulated, bored, or poorly nourished. On the other hand, when they are engaged in pleasurable interactions with the environment and with others and are able to control the amount of stimulation they experience, their brains are primed for making meaningful connections. Because play is child initiated, child controlled, and fun, it is an optimal context for learning.

The area of the brain that is the last to develop is the prefrontal cortex. This is the area that regulates behavior. Its basic functions are working memory (retaining information), inhibitory control (sometimes called self-discipline or self-regulation), and cognitive flexibility (changing perspectives). Termed *executive functions*, these processes are required for paying attention, planning, organizing, reasoning, making decisions, and solving problems. They are essential for success in school and beyond. The fundamental role of executive function is recognized beyond child development circles. A 2011 article by researchers Terrie Moffitt and colleagues, "A Gradient of Childhood Self-Control Predicts Health, Wealth, and Public Safety," says that children's ability to regulate their behavior predicts health, wealth, and public safety, regardless of intelligence or social class.

Dramatic play and other creative activities support the development of executive functions. In dramatic play, children use their working memories to represent what they know. They practice rule-bound behavior; they resist acting out of character, inhibiting responses that are inappropriate to that role. They adopt the perspectives of the person they are pretending to be. And in socio-dramatic play, they learn to switch their perspectives in response to their play partner's actions. These same functions are aspects of creativity: putting bits of information together in new ways and thinking outside the box.

COGNITIVE DEVELOPMENT

The relationships between brain development and cognitive development are complex. However, when teachers refer to cognitive development, they usually mean children's knowledge and thought processes. Dramatic play and other creative activities are closely intertwined with both. When children create mental images of their past experiences in dramatic play, they are processing information. As they construct imaginary worlds, they are engaging in "what if" thinking, the basis for hypothetical reasoning and problem solving. When they invent pretend situations with others, they are communicating ideas and learning from each other. They acquire new concepts that they subsequently test and revise. Pretending to be someone else enables them to learn about adult roles and careers. Engaging in dramatic play also allows them to apply what they have learned in one setting to a new situation. Acting out a pretend script requires mental planning and using the environment and materials on hand to serve particular purposes. For example, making a pretend cake requires remembering a series of steps and perhaps counting the right number of birthday candles. Buying food in an imaginary grocery store encourages the exploration, development, and application of math concepts and skills in meaningful ways. Constructing the physical frameworks for play helps children understand logical sequences, cause and effect, and spatial relationships. In the process, they continually evaluate their actions. It's common to see them revising their strategies, correcting each other, and even starting over from the beginning to enact a pretend scenario that didn't play out the way one or more of them thought it should.

Dramatic play and other creative activities help children make sense of the world around them and build on what they already know. At the same time, they are translating their thoughts and ideas into something tangible through their actions, the products they create, and the language they use. Those same processes are involved in everything they are required to do in school. Even so, academic success depends on more than cognitive development.

SOCIAL AND EMOTIONAL DEVELOPMENT

Acquiring social and emotional competence is a gradual process. In classrooms with dramatic-play centers, children participate in more complex social interactions than in any other area of the room. Through pretend play with others, they come to understand social and cultural norms and expectations. The rules that are implicit in peer play help them learn about and practice behaviors that underlie all social interactions. These include sharing, taking turns, communicating, and cooperating. In the process, children have opportunities to understand other peoples' intentions, desires, needs, and feelings. That ability to take another person's perspective is at the heart of empathy. Socio-dramatic play also helps children learn to resolve conflicts through negotiation and compromise and to read the emotional states of others through their gestures and facial expressions. This in turn helps them become more competent social partners, build friendships, and develop a sense of belonging to the classroom community. Positive relationships with peers affect children's adjustment to and success in school. After all, children learn alongside and through their peers. Those who do not feel part of the group often have difficulty functioning well in school.

Socio-dramatic play also supports children's ability to regulate their behavior and postpone gratification. In play, their actions must be consistent with the roles they have adopted. For example, children who have trouble sitting still during story time are often able to do so when the play script calls for it.

If it is "nighttime," they must remain still, pretend to sleep, and control their impulses to wake up before it is "morning." The play scenario and their peers scaffold their self-regulation skills.

In addition to promoting social skills, creative play is also emotionally nourishing. It is an arena where children are able to cope with their emotions. When they are worried, frightened, or feeling powerless, they can safely explore and express these feelings through their play. Pretending to be a doctor or a parent allows children to switch from feeling out of control to being in charge. Drawing pictures of monsters makes them seem less scary. Becoming a superhero helps children feel big and powerful in a world where they actually are the opposite. Play also provides a safe outlet for expressing strong feelings and impulses, such as anger or aggression. The child hitting a stuffed animal that cries for attention is much more acceptable than hitting a new baby sister!

In dramatic play and the other creative arts, children explore ideas, make connections, and figure out how to do things independently. Making personally meaningful discoveries and creating something new are deeply satisfying to children. The expressive arts nurture children's sense of self and are integral to their eagerness to learn.

LANGUAGE AND LITERACY DEVELOPMENT

Symbolic representations take many forms: talking, writing, dramatic play, and other forms of creative expression. Dramatic play and language have a reciprocal relationship; dramatic play fosters language development at the same time that language supports play. Children use language to communicate meaning. Even when they are playing by themselves, they often engage in private speech or self-talk, which serves to amplify and guide their behavior. In socio-dramatic play, children talk with each other to plan, organize, and structure their play outside the play frame. They explain what they want to do or are doing, give commands, and ask and answer questions. Then, within the play itself, they continue to practice conventional speech as well as situation-specific language using the vocabulary, register, and tone that are part of the roles they are enacting. Fire fighters speak differently from restaurant servers who speak differently from family members. We have all heard children reproduce adult speech with all the richness and color that it can contain—sometimes alarmingly so!

Language sustains imaginary roles. It also enables children to hear themselves from the "outside," to sense the conversations taking place between themselves and the person whose role they are playing. The language they use in dramatic play helps build effective speech and communication skills in individually meaningful ways.

The scenarios children act out in dramatic play have a story narrative. Younger preschoolers usually begin by representing familiar sequences of actions in their daily lives, such as cooking or driving. They progress to acting out more imaginative scripts and themes based on increased understandings, interactions, and exposure to books and screen media. High-quality dramatic play reveals children's knowledge that story elements include a beginning, middle, and end. For example, shopping involves looking for items you need, paying a salesperson for them at the checkout counter, and taking them with you in a bag. Snow White eats the poison apple, falls asleep, and waits until the prince awakens her.

Dramatic play is particularly important for children whose home language is other than English. Their English-speaking peers and the play context itself naturally support their acquisition of English, both in spoken and written

forms. The informal and nonthreatening atmosphere of play helps them build confidence as they learn new words, practice oral-language skills, and express themselves creatively. It both motivates and supports language development.

Socio-dramatic play is an especially powerful context for supporting literacy development. When literacy materials are available, pretend play is enriched and children use their developing skills in authentic reading and writing behaviors. They "write" messages, make signs, and "read" books and labels as they purposefully apply emergent literacy skills. As is true for all expressive and receptive language skills, making and interpreting written symbols through play helps build and strengthen the neural connections in the brain that are associated with literacy.

Other forms of creative expression also support language and literacy because they too involve using symbols to make meaning. For example, the marks, scribbles, and figures in children's drawings are visual symbols for their thoughts. Children will often "read" their drawings or talk enthusiastically about the stories they tell. Drawing is an emergent form of writing because it involves visual perception as well as perceptual and fine-motor skills. Children first begin to write by "drawing" print. They make letter-like forms (lines and circles) and then incorporate particular letters in their drawings. Eventually, they may cover an entire page with repeated letters and words.

Musical activities help children develop auditory perception and phonological memory, both of which are closely related to language and literacy. Children respond to the sounds and rhythms of language in music. They become aware of rhyming patterns and alliteration. Chants, rhymes, and songs make it easy to remember words. We're all familiar with children proudly singing "The Alphabet Song" and how easy it is for us to remember song lyrics when other information is easily forgotten.

Movement, too, is a form of communication and self-expression that aids language and literacy. When children actively move, they are orienting themselves in space. Spatial orientation is necessary for recognizing and forming letters. Movement and dance can also help children internalize vocabulary words such as *gently*, *quick*, *under*, *around*, and *through*.

PHYSICAL DEVELOPMENT

Children develop, practice, and refine their physical skills in all sorts of play activities. Dramatic play is no exception because physical actions are essential parts of it. No matter where their play occurs, children must be able to command their bodies within that space. Doing so may require perceptual motor

control, spatial and distance awareness, balance, and coordination. Different spaces, equipment, and materials require different kinds of physical responses. Pretending a climbing structure is a castle encourages more gross-motor skills than feeding a baby does. But even when children's play is less active, there are many opportunities to develop fine-motor skills. Putting on dress-up clothes entails managing snaps, buttons, and ties. Choosing and putting away play materials involves eye-hand coordination and visual discrimination skills. Dramatic play naturally encourages physical development. It also motivates children to develop and use self-help skills. The same can be said of other creative activities, depending on their physical aspects.

DRAMATIC PLAY AND "ACADEMICS"

If you are now teaching, you know that learning standards are the main driving forces in schools today. Preschools are no exception. Whether they are termed *guidelines*, *frameworks*, *foundations*, or *core curriculum*, they define expectations for what children should know and be able to do. Some standards are nationwide, such as the Head Start Learning and Development Framework; others have been developed by individual states with input from early childhood educators. Even though there are variations, most early learning standards outline key competencies that predict children's future success. These include foundational cognitive, social-emotional, language and literacy, and physical skills, as well as basic understandings related to mathematical and scientific thinking, social studies, and the arts. Despite a focus on play-based curriculum in many of these standards, they are sometimes interpreted as a way to push down curriculum and expectations from higher grades because teachers are accountable for addressing, measuring, and reporting outcomes.

A number of states' early education standards also include separate domains termed "Approaches to Learning." They indicate that active and persistent engagement in play, imagination, problem solving, and joyfulness are important competencies in development and learning. Creative play doesn't guarantee children will develop these dispositions, but without adequate opportunities to engage in self-selected and self-regulated activities, it is less likely they will.

Creative play works in concert with other learning activities to support development. As Lilian Katz writes in her preface to the 2013 *Illinois Early Learning and Development Standards*, creative play can "strengthen and support young children's intellectual dispositions and their innate thirst for better, fuller, and deeper understanding of their own experiences." Intellectual dispositions include engaging in extended interactions, taking initiative, applying emerging skills in purposeful ways, feeling a sense of belonging to the group, and experiencing satisfaction in individual endeavors and accomplishments. The main goal, according to Katz, should be helping children "acquire academic skills in the service of their intellectual dispositions and not at their expense."

Kindergarten teachers are well aware that dispositions like these and others that are supported by play-based activities are integral to children's success in school. When they are asked what qualities they hope children entering their classrooms will have, they often mention eagerness to learn and being able to self-regulate, follow directions, and work as part of a group. Teachers also hope they will be able to communicate their needs and desires verbally and be sensi-

tive to other children. These readiness skills arguably are more important than letter and number recognition because they directly relate to how teachable children are.

Dramatic play and creative activities encourage the underlying competencies and approaches to learning that ready children for the future.

CHAPTER
3

Supporting Dramatic Play
and Creative Expression

Understanding the central roles of dramatic play and other forms of creative expression in children's development and school readiness is one thing. Facilitating meaningful engagement in these activities is quite another. If this is your goal, your principal role is preparing an environment that is conducive to these activities through creating physical spaces, scheduling and managing time effectively, and providing materials and equipment.

SETTING THE STAGE FOR PURPOSEFUL PLAY

The environment you create communicates powerful messages to children about what they can and should do. Just like the mud puddle that beckoned the three-year-old to jump in, the physical setting and materials within it influence children's actions, involvement, and learning. That is why the environment has been called "the third teacher." It is also a critical variable in how children and teachers alike feel and interact with each other. Think about your reactions when you enter a new space. This might be a public building,

a friend's home, or another teacher's classroom. Do you feel comfortable or ill at ease? Do you recognize things that are familiar, or does everything seem foreign? Are your eyes drawn to things you're curious about, or is there nothing that sparks your interest? Do you know where to go or are you confused? Do you want to spend time in this space or are you ready to leave? As an adult, you are probably less impressionable and better able to control your reactions to different kinds of environments than most young children can. For that reason, these are important questions to ask when we design environments where children grow and learn.

The environment can also either support or hinder children's positive behavior. When they are actively engaged in interesting and developmentally appropriate activities, behavior problems are less likely. Environmental designs that provide clear boundaries, adequate room for particular activities, easy movement within the area, and private spaces help children manage their behavior.

Well-designed, welcoming, and stimulating environments with a mixture of familiar and novel materials encourage children's sense of security as well as their engagement in high-quality play. Knowing children well—their age-related and individual characteristics and needs as well as their interests and cultural and language backgrounds—is central in planning appropriate spaces that encourage sustained dramatic play and other creative activities. This includes ensuring equal access for all children, including those with physical disabilities.

CREATING DRAMATIC-PLAY CENTERS

Your classroom may already have an area for dramatic play. In many early childhood settings, these areas are called the *home living center* or *housekeeping area*, indicating the kinds of play activities they promote. They are common because they reflect children's experiences at home and in their families. Cooking and caring for babies are activities to which young children can easily relate. These centers encourage children to take on family roles and act out familiar actions. Younger preschool-age children and girls in particular tend to be drawn to these themes, but older preschoolers and boys are often less attracted, especially when other activity options are available. If we want all children to benefit from sustained dramatic play, we need to create dramatic-play centers that are gender neutral and reflect children's increasing experiences and interests outside their homes.

Consider the following as you plan an engaging dramatic-play center.

- **Designate a space.** Given the fundamental role of dramatic play in fostering learning, every early childhood classroom should have a permanent space dedicated to it. Whether this space is a corner of the room or a center with a distinct entrance, it should be separated from other areas by either visual or physical boundaries. Low shelves, bookcases and other furniture, and sheets draped from the ceiling can help define the space. Even colored tape on the floor will set this area off from other parts of the room.

- **Make room for four to six children to play together**. Adequate space for children to arrange and share props, put on clothing, and move about without getting in each other's way encourages cooperation and helps prevent conflicts. Crowding often causes irritability, angry outbursts, and disagreements. There should also be enough room so furniture can be rearranged and bigger items such as a tent or large box can be added. Too much space can result in solitary or parallel play or in overly energetic activities.

- **Provide proximity to the block center.** Locate the dramatic-play and block centers next to each other to enhance interaction among children and to enrich play. Block constructions can be used as dramatic-play props. Clothing and other materials from the dramatic-play area can inspire children to build their own environments out of blocks. In classrooms where these two centers are separated, it is quite common to see boys gravitate toward the block center and girls toward the dramatic-

play center, reinforcing stereotypic gender-based play and diminishing their range of experiences and learning opportunities.

- **Provide adaptable furniture and equipment**. Multipurpose, child-sized furniture helps define the space, provides storage, and supports play. A table with chairs, some low shelves, a freestanding pegboard with movable hooks, a full-length unbreakable mirror, a stove/oven, a sink, and a cupboard are practical and versatile pieces that can be moved around according to the theme. It is better to equip the center with a few durable pieces of furniture rather than many pieces that won't stand up to repeated use. However, when wooden or vinyl items are not available, you and the children can create less permanent furniture out of sturdy cardboard boxes or corrugated cardboard. Ideas and instructions for making cardboard dramatic-play furniture can be found on the Internet.

- **Offer visual appeal.** Attractive centers are more likely to engage children than those that lack visual appeal. When you arrange beautiful materials with care, you simultaneously convey the importance of dramatic play and make the center more inviting. Provide enough materials to support four to six children in sustained dramatic play. Too many materials can result in clutter and distraction; too few can cause conflicts and abbreviated play episodes. You do not need to furnish duplicate items of everything since the goal is to encourage children to take on different roles. Even so, multiples of particularly popular items might be necessary.

  Consider the walls and ceiling. Add interest by displaying photos, charts, and other items related to the play theme at children's eye-level. Textured wall hangings and items hung from the ceiling also make the space more inviting and supportive of play. Be sure to check school policies about attaching materials to the walls and ceiling fixtures.

- **Supply open-ended materials.** Props are the loose parts or accessories that inspire creative play. Include materials that can be used in many ways. Open-ended props encourage imagination and problem solving because children can decide for themselves how to use them. For example, a plastic bowl and wooden spoon are far superior to a toy mixer. In addition to being a cooking utensil, the bowl can become a shopping basket, a hat, a stool, a drum, a nest, or a container for other loose parts. Conversely, the manufacturer of the toy mixer has already decided what children can and should do with it. Similarly, plain pieces of cloth can be used as capes, scarves, blankets, tablecloths, animal skins, or even roofs; whereas, commercial costumes are designed for a single purpose. There is wisdom in the common observation that children are often more interested in the box than the toy that came in it. The box can be anything that children imagine it to be. Manufactured toys, especially ones with electronic parts, tend to encourage exploration rather than dramatic play as children focus on making them move, beep, or light up. Better to supply simple and open-ended props that are much higher in play value. Children can combine and recombine them in their own ways to suit the play scenario. Dramatic-play centers stocked with a variety of open-ended, moveable elements, as well as ones related to the theme, enable children with different abilities and interests to make meaning and to acquire, apply, and practice skills.

- **Provide life-size materials**. Provide props that support different roles to encourage children to play together. Clothing is especially important. Putting on a hat, shirt, or shoes helps each child become someone or something else. Other life-size props—*macrosymbolic* items—that support your theme or can be used in many ways are much better than small, *microsymbolic* objects such as sets of small figures that children more often use alone. Real items as opposed to toy replicas are more authentic and usually more interesting to children. They also tend to be more durable. Talking on a real but broken telephone is more satisfying than using a toy phone. Real items enable children to engage in and learn about real-life situations. Materials that they can use simultaneously also work well. For example, a tent encourages children to camp together.

- **Encourage gender and cultural inclusiveness.** Include materials that appeal to both boys and girls and that reflect children's cultural experiences in their homes and communities. In addition, consider providing materials that represent a broad range of cultural backgrounds and people of different abilities and ages to increase children's understanding of diversity. These can include clothing, such as ponchos, dashikis, kimonos, and baseball caps; cooking equipment, such as a *metate y mano* (used for grinding corn or mashing ingredients), gourds, or chopsticks; and other items, such as eyeglasses without lenses or crutches. Display pictures of people of different ages, genders, and ability levels in their jobs to help set the stage for play. A wide variety of multicultural and gender-neutral materials help counteract cultural or gender stereotypes based on appearance or behavior.

• **Support emergent literacy and numeracy.** Include materials to support children's emerging literacy and numeracy skills. Dramatic play is enhanced when children engage in literacy behaviors and practice their mathematical understandings. It only takes a little ingenuity to provide props that help children apply literacy behaviors and use mathematic skills in authentic ways. For instance, notepads and markers, inkpads with letter and word stampers, old computer keyboards, and a telephone can be added to almost every dramatic-play center regardless of the theme. A calendar, coupons, recipe cards, magazines, eye exam charts, play money, scales, and clocks are examples of items that encourage both literacy and numeracy.

- **Offer easy management.** Make sure play props are ones children can manage without assistance. They should be accessible and arranged to make choices clear. Too much clutter and disorganization can make choosing items difficult. The ages and characteristics of children in your group will determine the kinds of materials that are most appropriate. Obviously, safety comes first. Items with sharp edges should never be included. Remove cords from appliances such as hairdryers or rice cookers. Increase supervision when children have access to anything requiring special care. While dress-up clothes encourage self-help skills, smocks rather than shirts with buttons may be more appropriate for the children. Pieces of fabric also work well. They can be used in many ways. Place small items in labeled containers, and indicate in other ways where materials belong on shelves to speed cleanup and make it easier for children to maintain the center independently.

- **Remember the outside!** Outdoor areas are also wonderful stages for children's dramatic play. Free movement in a large space with natural elements such as sand, dirt, and vegetation inspires children to act out imaginative scenarios. Maybe you have seen (or can picture) small groups of children under the climbing structure or in a quiet area of the playground acting out stories of their own invention, or larger groups of children incorporating playground apparatus and chase games into their more adventurous play scripts. Just as in the classroom, loose parts enhance children's play outside. Riding toys, sand equipment, and large items children can manage independently enable them to extend their themes. Adding tires, wood planks, traffic cones, and pieces of PVC pipe further encourage creativity and problem solving and enable children to create backdrops for their dramatic play. Playgrounds are especially appropriate settings for play themes related to outdoor environments: a day at the beach, a gas station/garage, archeology, or animal safari. If outdoor storage space is not available, keep props related to these kinds of themes in crates or baskets so they can be easily carried outside.

Sources for Materials

Obtaining props and other materials need not be expensive or difficult. Great materials come from many sources and are readily available. Thrift shops and garage sales are treasure troves of props. Secondhand shops usually have a good assortment of children's clothing. You can also find furniture and outgrown children's items at yard and moving sales. Check your own or a relative's closet, attic, or garage. You may be surprised what you find!

Recycled household items, such as empty food containers, boxes, and scrap materials, are often perfect for storage, construction, and collage. Along with packaging for store-bought items, they become props for children to use in their play. Businesses have surplus, scrap, sample, or discontinued items they often discard. Use these for storage or to make equipment, instruments, or props. Acknowledge any contributions you receive with a thank-you note and/or a post on your bulletin board or newsletter. Sources for usable discards include the following:

- Appliance stores and moving companies—large sturdy boxes to create boats, castles, cars, spaceships, and puppet stages

- Carpet stores—rug samples or end pieces for dramatic-play centers and to dampen noise in music centers

- Fabric stores—cardboard from bolts of fabric (for clipboards, artwork mats), remnants and scrap notions

- Frame shops—matte board scraps

- Grocery stores—boxes of different sizes, paper bags, store displays, and storage containers for bulk food

- Kitchen and bath supply stores—mosaic tile pieces and linoleum squares

- Locksmiths—keys

- Lumberyards, hardware stores, cabinet/furniture makers or high school wood shops—wood scraps

- Medical offices—tongue depressors, disposable masks and bandages

- Paint and wallpaper stores—books of wallpaper samples, cardboard paint buckets, paint stirrers, and color samples

- Plumbing and builders supply stores—small lengths of PVC pipe and fittings

- Printing/copy shops—Scrap paper of different weights, colors, and textures

- Restaurants—corks and menus

- Shoe stores—shoe boxes

- Telephone and cable companies—colorful, easily bendable wire

- Upholsterers—scrap fabric and foam pieces

Families are often willing to donate items for the classroom. Send a wish list early in the year or as you develop a particular theme. These requests often result in wonderful materials for creative activities. Families have a vested interest in supporting their children's learning experiences, and this is a relatively easy way for them to do that. You will find an example of a wish list in Appendix D.

Homemade items or donated materials are often just as rich in play value as commercial ones. Besides being no- or low-cost, they model your resourcefulness and creativity for children and families. You can also invite family members to make equipment and props. If you or your school provides the raw materials and guidelines, parents are often willing to sew smocks, make puppets, or build cardboard or wooden furniture. They can also save you time by collecting surplus items from local businesses.

Materials and Equipment for Dramatic-Play Centers

Adaptable pieces of equipment and multiuse props support a variety of themes and are good additions to any dramatic-play center. Additional theme-specific props enhance the appeal and functionality of the center. There should be enough materials for four to six children to play together.

- Large versatile items
  - Bench
  - Easel(s) to display signs
  - Freestanding pegboard with hooks for hanging clothing, hats, and other props
  - Full-length unbreakable mirror
  - Indoor climbing structure that can be covered and converted into a number of structures (space ship, castle, drive-through restaurant window)
  - Kitchen furniture (sink-stove unit and cupboard)
  - Large blocks for children to use to create their own spaces and "furniture"

- Low shelves that provide easy access to props and can divide the physical space
- Table and chairs
- Trifold display panel

- Multipurpose props
  - Baskets and containers of various sizes for organizing small items and for children to use to gather play materials
  - Blankets
  - Clothing that children can manage independently and that is not oversized
  - Computer keyboard
  - Dolls and stuffed animals
  - Eyeglasses without lenses
  - Plain pieces of cloth
  - Purses and wallets
  - Steering wheel
  - Telephones
  - Nonbreakable hand mirror

- Literacy props
  - Art supplies, such as blank paper, pencils, and crayons to create signs and posters
  - Clipboard
  - Dry-erase board with markers

- File folders

- Generic signs such as Open/Closed or Exit/Enter

- Index cards and card file box

- Ink pad and letter or word stamps

- Sticky notes

- Mathematical and science props

  - Analog clock

  - Calculator

  - Calendar

  - Cash register or money box, play money, credit cards

  - Instrument/control panel with numbered dials

  - Magnifying glass

  - Measuring tape and ruler

  - Measuring cups

  - Scale

  - Tickets

  - Telephone

  - Watch

CREATING ART CENTERS

Creative art activities can be completed anywhere, but since art is so closely linked to children's communication, critical thinking, problem solving, and conceptual development, it is important to have a permanent area designed especially for it. An art center enables children to use and develop these skills every day as they plan and complete their own projects. It fosters their independence and responsibility. It also promotes their aesthetic sense and appreciation for the art of other individuals and cultures. It is your classroom's art studio.

As you plan your art center, consider what would make you want to dive into it yourself. How can you arrange the space to provide inspiration? How might you set up materials to excite participation? Would you want to create something with these materials? Is it clear where you can work on your own project?

Well-planned art centers usually function by themselves if they include the following elements.

- **Visual appeal:** Just like dramatic-play centers, art centers that are inviting and well organized engage children and make it clear what they can do. A table and easels to work on and low shelves with an array of accessible

materials tell them that this is a place where they can choose how to express themselves. Prints, posters, and calendars of fine art along with children's own artwork provide interest and inspiration. Bright light and colors add to the aesthetic appeal of the center.

- **Practicality:** An art center is a workshop where children's creative endeavors can sometimes be messy. Close proximity to a water source and surfaces that are easily cleaned are necessary. Keep newspapers and plastic sheets (shower curtains, plastic tablecloths, painters' drop cloths) on hand. These can be taped to the floor. Store wet and dry materials in separate areas. Place easels away from high-traffic areas. Hang smocks or adult shirts cut down to size on hooks to encourage children's independence in keeping their clothes clean. Provide drying racks for wet paintings or unfinished projects, to organize the center and to keep children's work accessible. Drying racks can be made from heavy cardboard or Masonite shelves supported by tiers of bricks or blocks. Use mats or trays to define areas for children to work and keep materials within reach. Linoleum tiles are especially good for use as a base in sculpting, molding, and creating heavier constructions and make it easier to move wet or incomplete projects out of the way. Individual workspaces have additional benefits of drawing children's attention and inviting their participation.

- **Child-centered activities:** Ensure children are able to use available materials to express themselves in their own way. The processes they use and anything they create should be unique, rather than attempts to re-create a predetermined product based on an adult model. You may need to introduce new materials to the entire class and model how to use particular tools. But posting examples of finished products or providing precut pieces for children to assemble denies them opportunities to experiment and express themselves freely without imposed expectations. This child-centered approach tells children that each of their ideas has intrinsic value.

- **Variety of open-ended materials:** Art supplies by their nature are open ended. By contrast, coloring book pages, tracing patterns, cut-and-paste, or dot-to-dot sheets are not appropriate. These kinds of materials are designed for a specific purpose by an adult or publishing house. They may help develop fine-motor control or eye-hand coordination, but they do not encourage children's creative expression. Categories of open-ended materials include paper (construction, newsprint, coffee filters, paper plates), tools for making marks (markers, crayons, pencils), tools for cutting (scissors, hole punches), materials for attaching (glue, staples, fasteners), materials for modeling (playdough, clay, and modeling tools), materials for painting and making prints (watercolors, tempera, brushes, and other tools), and bits and pieces for collage or assemblages (fabric, yarn, wallpaper, items from nature, wood scraps). The variety of art materials is practically unlimited. Stock your art center with these kinds of basic materials so children can choose among several options. But remember that too many choices can be overwhelming. There is also no need to change materials too often. Children need time to explore the physical properties of materials, experiment with them, and become skillful using them.

- **Adequate space:** Provide enough space for children to work on large projects and for several children to work at the same time without getting in each other's way. Children's creative processes do not always conform to classroom schedules. They may need to work on projects over time. If there is space for unfinished work, children can return to it until they decide it is finished. If shelf space won't accommodate a number of children's incomplete creations, their work can be kept on lunch trays and stacked on carts or drying racks. You may find that cubbies made from cardboard also serve this purpose well.

- **Order and organization:** Children are more productive when their environments are predictable and when they know where to find materials. Even though an emphasis on neatness can stymie children's creative expression, a space that is too disorganized can cause confusion and make it hard for them to focus. Disorganization also limits the center's appeal and can dampen your enthusiasm to provide art experiences in the first place. A simple organizational plan will help corral materials, encourage children's responsibility in maintaining the center, and make cleanup easier. Group and store papers and similar materials on low shelves. Label clear containers for tools and small supplies. Label spaces on shelves where materials belong with pictures, print, or hot-glued samples of the actual items. When every item has a place where it belongs, an art center functions efficiently. Children can access supplies independently and return them to their proper places when they're finished using them.

Highlight particular items by placing them in the center of the table to attract children's attention and help them make connections, explore and experiment. This is especially important if you have introduced particular activity choices or demonstrated tools to the group. Even though you have set out several kinds of materials, children should still feel free to add to or replace them with others they find more appealing.

- **Beyond the classroom walls:** As is true for dramatic play, the outdoors is a wonderful place for expressive art activities. Children can paint walls and playground equipment with water, use chalk on the sidewalk or blacktop, and create murals on paper taped to fences or suspended from clotheslines. Some particularly messy activities are best suited to the outdoors, such as painted feet prints and spray-bottle watercolor paintings. Picnic tables make good workspaces for children to use any materials brought outside on trays from the art center. Displaying children's creations outdoors enhances the child-centeredness and interest.

Materials and Equipment for Art Centers

A variety of drawing, painting, modeling, sculpting, collage, and construction tools and materials invite children to explore possibilities, problem solve, and express their ideas in two- and three-dimensional forms.

- Equipment
  - Adhesive cork tiles to create a display board
  - Drying rack(s)
  - Easels
  - Chalkboard
  - Cubbies for artwork
  - Low shelves
  - Table and chairs
  - Wheeled utility cart

- Reusable art supplies
  - Assorted painting tools (paintbrushes of various sizes, toothbrushes, sponges, droppers or pipettes)
  - Cafeteria trays
  - Carry all (plastic divided container)
  - Children's scissors (right- and left-handed)
  - Chopsticks for mixing paint
  - Containers to organize supplies (frozen juice, coffee, vegetable, and large popcorn cans; plastic tubs, and boxes)
  - Clipboards

- Drop cloths, shower curtains, plastic tablecloths

- Hole punches

- Kitchen tools for mixing and printing

- Linoleum squares for work surfaces and clay boards

- Modeling tools (forks, rolling pins)

- Muffin tins or Styrofoam egg cartons to hold paint

- Pie pans

- Rubber stamps and ink pads

- Rulers

- Screens for screen painting

- Smocks, child-size aprons, or shirts cut down to size

- Spray bottles (to wet watercolor paper or dilute paint)

- Stapler

- Whisk broom and child-sized brooms and dust pan

- Consumable art supplies

  - Assorted collage materials: fabric and paper scraps, wallpaper, sandpaper, yarn, gift wrap, tissue paper, ribbon, trim, buttons, stickers, beads, cotton balls, and other textured materials

  - Assorted craft supplies: wiggly eyes, feathers, foam shapes, glass gems, and pompoms

  - Bingo markers/daubers

  - Chalk

  - Clay

- Coffee filters

- Craft sticks or tongue depressors

- Crayons: regular and multicultural

- Egg cartons

- Glue

- Hangers

- Markers: regular and multicultural

- Natural items: seedpods, pinecones, shells, dried flowers, stones, and leaves

- Paint: powdered or liquid tempera paint, fingerpaint, liquid or cake watercolors, and acrylic paints

- Paper towels

- Pastels

- Pencils

- Paper in different sizes, colors, textures

- Paper plates

- Paste

- Pipe cleaners/chenille stems

- Playdough

- Recycled items: boxes, bottle caps, corks, and Styrofoam pieces

- Shells

- Tape

CREATING MUSIC CENTERS

Music and movement are integral to every early childhood program. Song games and creative dance are often woven into activities that take place in open spaces in the room during circle time and other whole-group gatherings. Adequate space is necessary for children in the group to move freely. Music centers, on the other hand, are smaller spaces where children can listen to music and creatively use musical materials and movement to express themselves independently.

Here are some considerations to help you plan an engaging music center.

- **Offer visual appeal.** Music centers that include interesting materials in an uncluttered environment are inviting and engaging. Put an assortment of instruments and other sound-making materials on low shelves or hang them from pegs. Display photos of people from different cultures playing instruments and dancing, and display posters related to music to indicate this center is designed for musical exploration and expression. Post words and musical scores to children's favorite songs.

- **Incorporate practicality.** To ensure that sound from the music center does not disturb other classroom activities, separate this center from quiet areas of the room. Sound-absorbing materials such as carpeting, floor pillows, and fabric hung on the walls and from the ceiling help to dampen noise. Include headphones and provide musical instruments that are not unduly noisy. A table draped on three sides with heavy fabric makes an inviting cave in which to explore musical sounds. Keep small items in containers and indicate with labels, contact paper cutouts, and/or photos where everything belongs. Since music demands movement, make sure there is enough space for several children to express themselves through dance.

- **Provide a variety of instruments.** Expose children to different types of music and musical instruments to expand their appreciation for musical styles beyond current popular culture. Provide a variety of musical instruments to encourage children to experiment with the musical sounds they make. In the process, they will be developing listening skills, improving coordination, and gaining understanding of rhythm and the ways music is made. Make sure children can manage most of the materials with minimal guidance. Whenever possible, invest in high-quality instruments that will last for years. Augment these with other sound-making materials such as shakers made from beans in sealed containers, oatmeal-box drums, rubber-band guitars, and sandpaper blocks. Include instruments from a variety of cultures to increase appreciation for different cultural heritages. Some types to consider are thumb harps from Africa, maracas and rain sticks from Latin America, finger cymbals from the Middle East, *den-den daikos* (pellet drums) from Japan, and ukuleles from Hawaii. You may even wish to provide a small keyboard with color-coded notes and song cards to encourage children to play familiar tunes. Add charts or picture songbooks to give children further opportunities to connect written symbols with music.

- **Offer additional materials.** Children move to music instinctively as they integrate it in their play. Add a container with a few props such as scarves and streamers and a full-length nonbreakable mirror to inspire children to dance to the music. If possible, locate the music and dramatic-play areas close together so children can choose dramatic-play props and clothing to further express themselves through music and dance.

- **Provide sound equipment.** Add a CD or tape player that children can operate independently along with child-size earphones. They will be able to choose songs and instrumental music from different genres and cultures that are most meaningful. Include picture books with musical themes for them to "read" to complement the experience.

- **Bring music out to the playground.** Outdoor environments are better than indoor spaces for some types of sound play. Examples of homemade musical instruments that can be housed outside include music walls with sound-making materials attached to them, chimes made from metal utensils or PVC pipes suspended from trees, and large drums made from overturned buckets or metal washtubs. Props from the indoor music center along with taped recordings and teacher facilitation will further enhance children's creative expression through music and movement when they are outside.

Materials and Equipment for Music Centers

Well-stocked music centers encourage children to explore, respond to, and experience the joy of creating and moving to their own music. They also support children's perceptual skills and appreciation for different kinds of music. Some of the possibilities include those listed below.

- Equipment
  - CD players with headphones
  - Floor pillows
  - Full-length nonbreakable mirror
  - Labeled baskets or other containers for smaller items
  - Low shelf to display materials
  - Small stage area
  - Tape recorder with headphones
- Musical instruments
  - Autoharp
  - Bells: hand, cow, cluster, jingle, wrist
  - Castanets
  - Drums

- Finger cymbals
- Maracas
- Rain sticks
- Rhythm sticks
- Sandpaper blocks
- Shakers and rattles
- Small electronic keyboard
- Tambourine
- Tone block
- Triangle
- Ukulele
- Xylophone and mallets

- Additional materials
  - Books with song lyrics
  - Conductor's baton
  - Flashlights or fiber-optic lights
  - Large doll to dance with
  - Microphones, broken or functional
  - Nontraditional sound-making materials: bubble wrap and kitchen tools

- Paper and pencils or markers for writing music

- Overhead projector and screen or sheet for shadow dancing

- Scarves or streamers

- Sheet music

MANAGING TIME

The amount of time we devote to particular activities indicates how important we think they are. If we value creative play as a fundamental medium for children's development and learning, we need to schedule ample time for it. It takes time for children to become fully engaged in high-quality play. In socio-dramatic play, they must decide together on a theme, negotiate roles, and gather props before they begin to pretend. Setting up their play can sometimes be a relatively quick process, particularly if children know each other well, but becoming fully absorbed in carrying it out takes much longer. Without adequate time, they are more likely to explore and to imitate adult roles and popular media characters rather than to collaborate to create their own stories. Full engagement in other creative activities also requires ample time. Children must first make choices, find materials and figure out how to manage them before they even begin to express themselves. Since the creative process is different for each child, they need to be able to work at their own individual pace. One child may use broad strokes to paint a self-portrait in ten minutes, while another child may take thirty minutes to paint the fine details of the design on his shirt. If children feel rushed or pressured, it is unlikely they will benefit from the learning opportunities provided by personally meaningful creative activities. They need time to use materials and make connections in their own way.

For these reasons, longer blocks of time are more conducive to high-quality dramatic play and other creative activities than shorter, interrupted periods. Forty-five to sixty minutes of uninterrupted play supports in-depth and purposeful play along with self-direction and self-expression. This amount of time enables children opportunities to take initiative, follow through with their plans, and develop independence. It allows them to shift to a new activity when they have finished with the first, and it also is easier to manage because there are fewer whole-group transitions.

In early childhood programs, time for creative play goes by different names such as center activities, choice time, and work-play time. Consistent daily routines help children feel secure and develop independence. However, within the period scheduled for creative activities, there should be enough flexibility so children can choose the areas or centers where they want to play. You can introduce activity choices for the day during the opening group or morning meeting and ask children what they plan to do. This supports their ability to take initiative, organize a plan, and self-regulate, all of which are essential executive functions.

When the same materials and activity choices are set up in a center for an entire week, all children have opportunities to play there. This enables children to choose and remain in particular centers for a sustained period of time. Weekly plans also allow them to return to activities that are particularly engaging or to continue working on their creations. On other days in the week they can spend focused time in other centers. Conversely, rotating children through each center every day diminishes their opportunities to develop the executive functions listed above. It also makes in-depth engagement in activities less likely. Scheduling a particular amount of time in each center before children must move on to the next center may be convenient for teachers, but doing so means some children will have completed activities while others have only just begun. Children's interests and engagement should govern scheduling, rather than the clock.

These examples of daily schedules highlight adequate time for children's dramatic play and other creative activities.

Half-Day Preschool Schedule

8:45–9:00	Arrival
9:00–9:20	Large group (opening conversations and planning)
9:20–10:20	Center activities
10:20–10:30	Cleanup
10:30–10:45	Large group (stories, songs, sharing projects)
10:45–11:15	Small groups (snack followed by teacher-child initiated activities)
11:15–11:45	Outdoor play with departure from the playground

Full-Day Pre-K or Kindergarten Schedule

7:00–8:00	Before-school care
7:45–8:15	Arrival onto the playground
8:15–8:30	Morning meeting
8:30–11:00	Work-play time
11:00–12:00	Lunch followed by recess
12:00–1:00	Whole- and small-group activities
1:00–2:30	Work-play time
2:30–3:00	Recap and preparation for departure
3:00	Pickup
3:00–6:00	After-school care

Full-Day Kindergarten Schedule

7:45–8:15	Arrival
8:15–8:45	Whole-group opening
8:45–10:30	Morning activity time (independent learning centers, small-group work with teacher)

10:30–10:45	Share and review
10:45–11:15	Lunch
11:15–11:45	Outdoor recess
11:45–12:30	Quiet time (shared reading experiences, journal writing)
12:30–12:45	Whole-group music and movement
12:45–1:45	Afternoon activity time (independent learning centers, small-group work with teacher)
1:45–2:15	Specials
2:15–2:45	Afternoon meeting (reflections, wrap-up, pack up, dismissal)

USING TECHNOLOGY APPROPRIATELY

Children are surrounded by technology. They are likely to see their parents using the Internet and texting friends on their phones, older children playing video games, scanners in the grocery store, and computers in the pediatrician's office. Screen media is practically inescapable. While many of us have learned to use these kinds of technology tools as adults, they are part of the fabric of young children's lives. Children take them for granted. They are interested in exploring and learning about them just as they are about other parts of their world.

The concern about technology for young children, even among chief executives of technology companies who limit their own children's use of it, is that exposure at too early an age or in excessive doses can diminish their real-world experiences. It can inhibit human interactions, reduce physical activities and hands-on experiences, and limit creative thinking. Perhaps, like me, you have seen two-year-olds sitting in the bottom of their parents' grocery carts glued to handheld devices rather than noticing and talking about all the things there are to learn about in a market. You might also be familiar with children who imitate the aggressive actions of video characters rather than invent their own dramatic-play scenarios, or who are more comfortable in the digital world than in the real world.

Professional organizations and early education experts agree that developmentally appropriate and meaningful technology can be integrated effectively into young children's learning experiences if it is used as a tool to stimulate conversations and interactions and to strengthen children's engagement in learning. The same may be said for playful and imaginative experiences: appropriate technology can encourage creative activities if it inspires new ways of playing and communicating ideas. It is up to you to decide when, how much, and what kinds of technology to use to inspire dramatic play and creative activities. If technological devices distract children from sustained creative expression, they should be used for other purposes or omitted altogether. For example, the sounds and virtual displays of some digital devices promote solitary exploration, divert children from creative activities, and interfere with ongoing classroom practices.

Any technology that is included in dramatic play, art, and music centers should enhance children's interactions with concrete materials and their peers. It should also give children new ways to express their own ideas. The rapid pace of innovations in technological devices and software may soon provide other appropriate additions to your centers. Use discretion as you weigh the benefits and drawbacks of incorporating these or other kinds of technology. Examples of technology tools you might consider adding to increase creative expression follow.

- Dramatic Play
  - Digital camera for children to take photos or videos of their play
  - Digital scale or calculator
  - Waiting-list form on a computer tablet

- Art Center
  - Digital cameras for children to photograph artwork
  - Interactive whiteboards with connections to a computer and projector
  - Open-ended drawing or paint program on a computer tablet
  - Overhead projector or document camera

- Music Center
  - Computer programs for making music
  - Digital camera to photograph and videotape music and dance
  - Digital microphone and CD player for children to record and listen to their songs
  - Electronic keyboard
  - Karaoke machine

There are many technology tools that can help you set the stage for play.

- Software programs make creating signs, labels, and other print props quick and easy.

- Some teaching-related websites include printables of signs and labels. Choose any you use with care, and avoid those that are prescriptive. Select ones that enhance children's experiences rather than make them less child-initiated and more instructive.

- Software can enable you and the children to create books of their artwork with their descriptions of it.

- Photos on teacher blogs provide ideas for setting up dramatic play, art, and music centers.

- An Internet search for images related to particular themes will yield photos to display that may inspire children's creative expression.

- Internet searches also will help you bring otherwise inaccessible pieces of music and videos of music and dance performances into your classroom.

- Photos or scans of children's artwork and audio/video recordings can be compactly stored, used in future projects, or added to portfolios.

For tips on using technology to communicate and illustrate the importance of creative play in children's lives, please see Involving Families on page 92.

PLANNING PLAY AND CREATIVE ACTIVITIES

Arranging inviting environments and provisioning them with open-ended materials are the first steps in promoting dramatic play and creative activities. Much of this stage setting takes place before children are present. But it doesn't stop there. After children arrive, there are many ways to encourage creative play. Some strategies support all children's play. Others are based on your understanding and observation of individual children.

- **Learn about children's interests.** Listen to their conversations and comments during group discussions. Watch what they do on the playground. This is where they often feel most free to structure their own activities. What they say and do will help you learn more about their interests and concerns and will give you ideas for especially relevant themes and activities. Children who make a campfire out of the sand or fill their bikes with gas know something about these processes. A camping or gas-station dramatic-play center will help them build on their understandings as they develop other skills.

- **Keep the atmosphere relaxed and free of risk.** When children feel their ideas and forms of expression will be accepted and valued, they are more likely to play and work freely and flexibly. When the atmosphere is risk free, they are able to experiment, innovate, and truly benefit from creative play. If they fear judgment according to a particular standard, they are apt to conform to the expectations of others.

- **Model playfulness and creative expression.** Your own attitude, approaches, and involvement can spark children's creativity. Talk about things you are curious about. Think out loud about possibilities. Show your excitement about learning to do new things. Laugh at your own silliness. Dance and sing with children, keeping in mind that they don't care what your voice sounds like or how gracefully you move. Your involvement and enthusiasm are what matter to them. Shut the door if this makes you more comfortable!

- **Provide background experiences.** Firsthand experiences are the raw material of creative play. They help children become familiar with themes and roles beyond their experiences with their families and with what they are exposed to through screen media.

- **Read and relate stories.** Whether read or told, stories trigger children's imaginations and inspire various kinds of symbolic representation. Ask children to provide sound effects or pantomime actions while you read. Encourage their engagement in creative play by using puppets related to the stories during group conversations or by reenacting story events all together. Ask them open-ended questions about story elements or characters' actions and feelings.

- **Invite guests to talk about their jobs or hobbies.** Include ones to which children might be particularly drawn: firefighter, veterinarian, bus driver, medical staff, or construction worker. Guests who wear uniforms or demonstrate equipment and those who engage children in pretend scenarios are particularly effective in prompting later dramatic play.

- **Plan excursions.** Trips beyond the classroom open the world to children and provide shared experiences. Back in the classroom, children process and draw upon this information in their play, art, music, and movement. There are many possibilities for excursions—some near at hand, others farther afield. Imagine how the trips listed here can be catalysts for dramatic play and other creative activities.

  - Walking trips within the school
    - Cafeteria or kitchen
    - Janitor's work room
    - Library
    - Office
    - School bus

  - Walking trips in the neighborhood
    - Community garden
    - Construction or roadwork sites
    - Fire station
    - Grocery store
    - High school music room

- Laundromat

- Library

- Neighborhood businesses (restaurant, bank, bakery, repair shop, garage)

- Field trips

  - Art gallery

  - Children's theater

  - City hall

  - Dance studio

  - Doctor's or dentist's office

  - Factory

  - Farm

  - Museum

  - Pet store

  - Plant nursery

  - Television or radio station

  - Transportation hub (airport, bus terminal, train station, harbor)

  - Veterinarian clinic

  - Zoo

- **Take advantage of the unexpected.** Unplanned events such as a thunderstorm, roadwork in front of the school, or a child's dog having puppies can capture children's imaginations and can be the basis for creative play. After talking with children about occurrences such as these, add props for dramatic play and related art and music materials to capitalize on the learning opportunities they provide. In these cases, you could add construction or veterinarian props, wood scraps, dry tempera paint and spray bottles, or rain sticks.

- **Plan with children.** Whenever possible, involve them in creating dramatic-play centers. Ask questions such as the following:

  - *How should we arrange the furniture?*

  - *What materials should we include or add?*

  - *Can you use things you have made as props?*

  - *Are there items you can bring from home?*

  Whenever children see their own ideas projected, their engagement is especially meaningful and satisfying. Families are also wonderful sources for authentic play materials, particularly those related to their own cultural backgrounds. Requests are an easy way to encourage their involvement and further connect home and school.

- **Introduce activities.** Talk with children about the materials you have placed in the centers. Build anticipation and excitement by asking questions about what they know about particular themes and by helping them plan what they will do. Demonstrate how to use new props or items that may be unfamiliar.

- **Establish center guidelines.** Help children understand simple rules for playing in each center. For example, "After using an item, put it back where it belongs." Children need to know what to do when materials and space are limited. They need guidelines for waiting, taking turns, and sharing. Certainly, talking with children about classroom ground rules and expectations is necessary. But visual cues help to reinforce them and support children's self-regulation. If there is room for only four children in a center, post a graphic of that number or include a pocket chart or hooks with a limited number of spaces for children to put their name cards to serve as a reminder. Sign-up sheets or a take-a-number system also can help children know when it is their turn to play. Trays provide personal workspace in the art center and eliminate conflict. Children will need you to model how these systems work and to be on hand as they learn to wait, take turns, and share.

- **Make time to watch.** Observe how children use materials and interact with each other. Ask yourself if additional or alternative props or tools would further encourage their participation. Do they need your support in entering ongoing play or getting started? Can you unobtrusively help them sustain their play to benefit most from it? Frequent observation will help you know how best to encourage their play.

FACILITATING CREATIVE PLAY

Your role as a stage manager consists of more than providing time, space, and materials. Some children will need gentle encouragement to become involved. Others will need guidance in playing well with others. You may also see occasions to help them engage in higher levels of sustained, cooperative, and meaningful play. Once play is under way, responsive interactions with children can enhance it and expand opportunities for learning. Even so, your goal should be for children to engage in creative play that they themselves select and structure. Interrupting or dominating an activity diminishes its benefit.

Deciding when and how to facilitate play begins with observing children's interactions and reflecting on the underlying causes of their behavior. Try to see things from their perspectives rather than your own. Listen to what they are trying to communicate and attempting to do. When you are not sure, ask them open-ended questions. Understanding the developmental characteristics, needs, and interests of each child will help you choose the least intrusive strategies to help him benefit most from creative play. How you support one child will be different from how you support another. Be particularly careful about using strategies that take ownership away from children. When this happens, play becomes an adult-led activity where children no longer control the process. The goal of any strategy is to help children take a step rather than you taking it for them. Being too quick to solve their problems robs them of rich and meaningful learning opportunities.

Strategies for facilitating play lie on a continuum from less to more teacher involvement, ranging from simply helping children plan their play to coaching them as they acquire specific skills. Your role as a facilitator will shift according to the situation and each child's involvement.

Roles in Facilitating Creative Play

The strategies you use can either be outside the play episode or inside the play itself. For example, asking children questions about what they are trying to do or adding materials are outside strategies. Being a coplayer is an inside strategy.

- **Planning assistant.** Helping children plan enriches the play of even the best players. After initially setting the stage for play, ask children what they intend to pretend or create. This might be a simple question such as, "What are you going to do today?" or it can become a conversation to guide their thinking about who they will play with, what materials they will need, and what might happen. Planning is part of the executive functions of organizing, reasoning, and making decisions. Children's responses will help you help them recognize and think through potential problems. They will also let you know if additional props or materials are needed or whether a center could be rearranged to accommodate their ideas. Encouraging children to plan ahead gives you opportunities to ask questions and make suggestions to further enhance their play.

• **Onlooker**. It is a true pleasure to observe children who are completely absorbed in well-developed play. You need do little to enhance it except watch from the sidelines and convey appreciation through your body language and perhaps a comment such as, "It looks like you're having fun," to show you value their play. When you are close by, children know they can ask for materials or assistance, allowing you to respond accordingly. Being an onlooker is different from letting play happen while you take care of other things. It requires your attention and availability. In the process you will learn more about children's development and know when interventions might enhance their learning. Do they need help communicating their ideas or cooperating with others? You

will also be able to assess how the spaces and materials you have provided are being used and can make needed adjustments. Are there enough materials for children to use? Are there too many? Can children manage them independently? Could adding new materials or tools enrich their play and self-expression when they return to the center on another day?

- **Offstage supporter.** Your role as an onlooker will tell you when interactions with children are warranted. There are two main reasons to intervene in children's play. One is to help facilitate or sustain it. The other is to mediate conflicts. In addition to enhancing creative play in general, interventions should be based on your goals for individual children. For example, if a child needs help with oral language, self-regulation, or persistence, creative play provides an excellent context for nurturing those skills.

- **Supporting and sustaining.** Well-considered questions and comments enhance and extend creative play and help children develop their ideas.
  - Keep the play going and give children new ideas or ways to think about what they're doing.
    - *What are you serving in your restaurant today?*
    - *This dog has hurt his paw. Can you take care of him?*
  - Suggest materials or different things to try.
    - *Here are some bandages for your patient.*
    - *Is this something you could use to make your sign?*

- Encourage children's collaborations.

  - *Mari, can you show Ngoc how you built that campfire?*

  - *Can you make another place at the table for Stevie?*

  - *Jorge, I see Tyrone is selling tickets to the movie. Would you like to buy one?*

- Offer direct assistance.

  - *It looks like you could use some help with that.*

- Show children ways of using materials or tools, but only when it is clear they need help gaining control.

  - *When you wipe the brush on the cup like this, it will be easier to make it stay where you want it to stay.*

- Amplify what children are doing.

  - *Mmmm. Your soup smells yummy. You've added rice and vegetables and chicken and salt. Are there enough bowls for you to serve your friends?*

- **Mediating conflicts.** Even in the most engaging environments, conflicts occur. Disagreements over materials and space are common in early childhood classrooms. Because young children are still developing language and self-regulatory skills, they can be quick to resort to force or threat. They may also exclude others who they think will disrupt their play. Give children time to try to work out problems that do not involve aggression. Doing so helps them gain valuable skills in conflict resolution and become responsible for their own behavior. However, immediate intervention is necessary when their actions or words hurt other children. Strategies to respond to inappropriate behavior and help children resolve disputes are specific to each situation.

- Reinforce classroom rules using the word *we*.
  - *At school we don't hit other children. We use our words.*
- Calm upset children. Go with them to a private place. Give them small things to play with such as stuffed animals or blocks until they are calm enough to return to playing with others. This is not the same as time out, which isolates children.
- Interpret children's actions and check for understanding.
  - *It looks like you need more room.*
  - *It looks like you both want to wear that hat.*
  - *You weren't finished yet with the yellow paint. Is that right?*
- Listen to each child. Ask questions to help them think through steps they can take to resolve the conflict by themselves.
  - *What have you done to solve your problem?*
  - *Is there something else you could try so that you're both happy?*
  - *What do you think would happen if you did that?*
- Support communication. After asking children what they want, help them express it in words others will understand.
  - *I need the blue crayon.*

• I want to make the torti-llas by myself.

• I can be the little sister.

• Help children connect their actions with the conse-quences of those actions.

> *• Caden, Twi fell and skinned her knee when you bumped into her. What can you do to make her feel better?*

• Give descriptive feedback to recognize and reinforce positive behavior. Your goal in any intervention should be to help children ac-quire the social and emotional skills to resolve con-flicts on their own. When they put their skills into practice, it is important to acknowledge what they have done.

> *• I heard you and Misha arguing about who would be the veterinarian. Your decision to take turns was a good idea.*

> *• You were kind to help April put her groceries back in the bag after you accidentally knocked it over.*

> *• You were helpful putting all the camping equip-ment away. That was a big job.*

- **Coplayer.** More active facilitation of children's play takes place inside the play frame. You may find natural openings to join in by taking on a minor role in the play script. This will allow you to enrich and enhance play from the inside through playing your part and modeling play behaviors. You might use language and actions to support individual children or make comments and introduce ideas to help sustain or even redirect play. For example, if you observe children imitating characters they have seen in the media, you can introduce new ideas to help change the story narrative. Instead of fighting the bad guys, superheroes can rescue and take someone who is hurt to the hospital. Instead of simply dressing up to "look pretty," princesses can care for the sick or protect others from danger. Your involvement adds to the complexity of the play scenario. Even so, it is very important to take cues from the children and not become a director. Children must remain in control and retain ownership of their play.

- Attract children to the center, offer security for those who are hesitant, and draw attention to particular materials.

- Invite a reluctant observer to join in.

  - *Manny, we're going out for pizza. Would you like to come, too?*

- Interpret the play script and model play skills such as sharing.

  - *We're giving our babies a bath but there's only one tub, so we have to share it.*

- Include different elements in the play scenario to extend it.

  - *I wish bakeries also made sandwiches. They would have more customers.*

- Introduce a new idea when play is in danger of falling apart.

  - *Someone's been hurt. Can you call an ambulance?*

- Broaden children's conceptions about "acceptable" activities for girls and boys.

  - FEMALE TEACHERS: *I need to wear a firefighter's hat to put out the fire.*

  - MALE TEACHERS: *I need to put on an apron to bake these cookies.*

- Model social norms and positive behavior.

  - *May I please have a turn after you are finished?*

  - *This baby is crying. I'm going to comfort him like this.*

- **Coach.** Less-experienced players or children with limited play skills may need help figuring out how to join ongoing play without disrupting it or being rejected.

  - Help children get started by clarifying activity or material choices.

    - *What are you ready for today—playing in the post office or painting?*

  - Teach children to ask, "How can I play?" instead of "Can I play?" This open-ended question encourages other children to think of ways the new child can be included. It is easier for them to say no to the latter question.

- Watch play from the sidelines with children and help them determine what the play theme is.
  - *What do you think they're doing?*
  - *Do you think they're playing hospital?*
  - *Are they selling tickets to the show?*
- Talk them through how they might contribute to it. Is there a role they can play, a prop they can add, or a way they can help? If necessary, model words to introduce their ideas.
- Help children acquire basic play skills. A small number of children may need direct practice enacting common play themes and sequences of actions with just you before you help them enter play with others. As their play partner, you can coach them as they acquire the social, emotional, and cognitive skills that will enable them subsequently to play with one or more of their peers

A Few Cautions

Play is fragile. Inappropriate interventions in children's play will disrupt it or end it altogether. When play becomes teacher directed rather than child centered, the resulting activity contradicts the freely chosen and intrinsically motivating characteristics of creative play. If children no longer control the action, they do not have the same opportunities to gain value from their play. They are not able to freely express themselves or develop the same kinds of basic skills that are vital for success in school and beyond: self-regulation, symbolic thinking, social and problem-solving skills, persistence, confidence in their abilities, and satisfaction in their accomplishments. Your goal should be to facilitate and extend well-developed creative play in the least intrusive ways so that it remains child initiated and child directed.

Things to avoid:

- Taking ownership of ideas away from children

- Stepping in to teach academic skills

- Being too quick to solve children's problems

- Correcting children's "mistakes"

- Giving unsolicited advice

- Imposing ideas on the processes children are using or the products they are creating when they are happy with how thing are going

- Giving directions

- Rigidly adhering to time schedules and strict routines

- Rushing children to finish

To avoid interrupting play, ask yourself: Who's in control? Whose ideas are guiding the play? Who's choosing? Whose version of experience is being portrayed?

MAKING PLAY VISIBLE

Capturing what children have done in words, images, or on video highlights learning through play. The benefits of doing so are many.

- You validate and honor children's endeavors and magnify their voices.

- You encourage them to revisit what they have done and to think about their experiences and how they have made sense of them. In other words, it helps them think about their own thinking to make further meaning.

- You inspire additional expression through language and more complex play.

- It enables you to understand and expand on their efforts.

- It helps you provide appropriate feedback and reinforcement for initiative, persistence, problem solving, innovation, and collaboration.

- It provides concrete evidence of the power of creative play to promote learning.

- It's easier to share children's learning through play with families, colleagues, and supervisors.

Different types of creative expression lend themselves to different kinds of documentation and display. Make anecdotal records—brief handwritten notes—of ways children are engaged in creative play. Photograph or video dramatic play episodes for children to review and talk about. Photograph children engaged in art projects to capture the processes they use. Whenever possible, take photos that tell a story. A series of photos of how play and creative expression evolve and the processes children use can help to make their thinking visible, both to themselves and to others. Record the songs they sing and the music they make for them to listen to and expand upon. Record or take dictation of their stories about their creative play episodes.

Dramatic Play

Post captioned images of play at children's eye level or exhibit the photos in the hallway for others to see. Add them to printed or electronic newsletters for families. Include them in children's portfolios or books documenting their development. Attach captions to explain the context for each image so that it conveys the importance and complexity of children's involvement and serves as a springboard for conversations.

Smart phone and computer tablet technology make it easy to record particular episodes of children's dramatic play on the spur of the moment. Reviewing these recordings with children sparks dialog, group planning, and extended creative expression.

Art

Display captioned photographs of children creating visual art as well as displays of what children have actually created. The way you handle children's artwork conveys how you value it. Mount two-dimensional pieces on a larger piece of construction paper; frame them inside file folders, meat trays, or shoe-box or gift-box lids; or place them in ring binders or staple them into booklets. Linoleum, Masonite, or cardboard squares provide a solid base and border for three-dimensional pieces. A mirror underneath or in back of the piece allows it to be seen from other viewpoints. Be sure to attach a description or, better yet, children's explanations for their work. You can also affix a note with a more detailed explanation of how each piece demonstrates children's growth.

Rather than posting all children's artistic creations made with the same media, consider selecting pieces in which children have been fully invested or ones that represent their learning. An area of your classroom can become an art gallery with artwork matted and hung on the walls and three-dimensional artwork exhibited on a shelf or table below. Send other artwork home or add it to children's portfolios. You can also mark off wall space for each child to display whatever she chooses.

Music and Movement

Photographs, audio recordings, and videos can capture children's music and movement expression. They delight in hearing their voices and music and seeing how they responded to sound with their bodies. As in other forms of creative expression, opportunities to revisit what they have done encourage thinking and planning skills and motivate further engagement.

INVOLVING FAMILIES

Families are your allies in facilitating children's creative play. They can provide materials, act as visiting experts, encourage play at home, or simply read school bulletins to learn more about play. Their involvement supports classroom activities and serves as an indirect form of parent education. Families' active engagement can take many forms.

- **Donating items:** Families are wonderful sources for classroom materials. Ask them to donate recycled household items or to canvas local businesses for surplus or discontinued items. A wish list will give them ideas for the kinds of materials that are appropriate for your classroom. Examples of the kind of wish list you might create are in Appendix D. If families contribute abundant materials, involve children in sorting items into different categories.

When children bring items from home, validate their contributions during group time. When culturally specific items such as chopsticks are donated, use that as an opportunity to foster cultural awareness. Acknowledge family contributions with special thanks in newsletters or bulletins.

- **Making materials:** You may have one or two parents who are handy with a sewing machine or hammer or who enjoy making crafts. They may even be pleased to receive an invitation to make props and equipment for your classroom. Give them the raw materials and simple directions. Parents with work and childcare responsibilities and those who lack transportation or are uncomfortable volunteering in your classroom may be especially willing to contribute their time and talents in these ways.

- **Visiting the classroom:** Ask parents and other family members to talk about their jobs and share special talents or hobbies with children. Parents whose work is the kind to which children can easily relate, such as police officers, nurses, mail carriers, bus drivers, or food preparers, are especially wonderful resources. Demonstrating what they do and the equipment they use gives children background information that inspires creative expression. Similarly, parents can show how they make, use, or collect items related to their avocations. They can also be an extra pair of hands helping in the art center, reading to children, or accompanying the class on excursions. In addition, an open-door policy serves as a standing invitation for parents and others to see for themselves the benefits of creative play.

- **Facilitating home-based creative play:** Use newsletters, bulletins, or school websites in families' home languages to help spread the word about the benefits of creative play. Include friendly suggestions about limiting children's exposure to screen-based media, particularly with violent or sexual content, and about the importance of providing time, space, and materials and the kinds of background experiences described earlier to stimulate playing to learn. Encourage families to pretend, create art, sing, dance, and make music with their children. Provide suggestions such as letting children dress like characters in their favorite books, make puppets from the fingers of old gardening or dishwashing gloves, or create collages from magazine pictures.

Send home materials to make creative play especially inviting. Place a few materials in a child-size backpack or ziplock bag to create a take-home dramatic play, art, or music kit. You can loan kits for a week or more, giving adequate time for in-depth engagement. The materials you include will encourage conversations and help family members build on children's concepts, skills, and intellectual dispositions. A dramatic-play kit can contain a favorite storybook, props related to the story, and a brief invitation to read the book and act out the story together. You can also send props that support a particular dramatic play theme. Shopping-related themes, such as grocery or shoe store, work well because of the different roles associated with them. Families will be able to incorporate household items to make play even more meaningful and fun.

Children may not have access to basic art materials such as crayons or scissors at home, let alone the kinds of art supplies listed earlier. They will be eager to take home a kit with an assortment of interesting art materials. They can combine these materials with ordinary household items for hours of creative learning. For a music and movement kit, include several handheld musical instruments, a conductor's baton, and a CD with rhythmic music or children's songs. You can also provide a book with a musical theme or song lyrics and perhaps ideas for making homemade instruments.

In any kits you send home, include an invitation to participate in creative activities. Be sure to add a brief explanation of what children can do with the materials, such as the following.

- Pretend to be one of the characters in the story.

- Take turns being the salesperson and customer.

- Draw what you see out your window.

- Make a card or gift for someone.

- Re-create a room in your house.

- Find items in your home that make different sounds.

- Clap, tap, and dance to the beat of the music.

Giving or loaning concrete creative play materials to families endorses children's creative expression and learning through play. It makes it easy for families to share in that process. It also enables parents to see for themselves the effectiveness of open-ended materials and the connections between creative play and their children's learning.

CHAPTER

4

Ideas for
Dramatic-Play Activities

Listen to children's conversations and observe their interactions to identify good themes for dramatic play. As you select themes, remember that children's play is rooted in what they have experienced firsthand. Here-and-now events such as a construction project in the neighborhood or family occupations or outings make good themes because children already have some background knowledge from direct experience. You can also plan themes related to seasonal events or favorite stories, just as you do in other areas of the curriculum. But if children's only understanding of a topic such as a farm is based on books and other secondary sources of information, their play will be less rich and meaningful than if they have visited a farm or live in farm country.

Keep in mind children's developmental levels. Appropriate themes for younger preschool-age children will likely relate to familiar home-based experiences, such as cooking, washing, and caring for younger children, because those are most closely tied to their lived experiences. As four- and five-year-olds' interests and

experiences in the wider world expand, themes with an away-from-home focus—
say a shoe store, post office, or veterinary clinic—become more relevant.

To stimulate children's imaginations, integrate creative dramatics into teacher-
guided activities. For example, when you read a story to children, ask them to
provide sound effects or to pantomime actions. Ask them to choose a puppet
from a basket and tell a story about it. Prompt them by beginning their
stories, "Once upon a time . . . ." Place a favorite storybook along with a few
props related to the story in your classroom library or dramatic-play center as
inspiration for children to act out the story in their own way.

Whenever possible, plan with children instead of just for them. Their involvement opens up possibilities you may not have thought of and makes learning
opportunities especially rich. One way to do this is to place a large appliance
box on its side in your dramatic-play center. Add a basket of hats and a few
open-ended materials, such as blankets, stuffed toys, a telephone, a purse and

wallet, a bowl, a few spoons, and a set of measuring cups. Watch what children do with these materials. Listen to their conversations about who they are and what they are doing. Build on their interests by adding appropriate equipment and props. You can also encourage them to suggest themes. Ask if they are interested in having their own restaurant or hospital. Find out how they think the dramatic-play center should be set up and what items they will need. Invite them to bring props from home or to create props themselves with materials you provide.

With these recommendations in mind, the ideas in this section are intended to support you in encouraging children's sustained dramatic play and creative expression. Choose from and adapt those that best fit your own situation and the children you teach. What is relevant and engaging to one group of children may not be as appropriate or interesting to another group. You know the children and circumstances best, so you be the judge.

The dramatic play themes that follow are only some of many possible themes as are the ideas for center arrangement, props, facilitating engagement, and related experiences. Even so, perhaps these suggestions will prompt your own creativity.

The center arrangement for your dramatic-play area will depend on your space, furnishings, and the children's characteristics and interests. You may already have furniture and equipment, such as a kitchen center, a puppet theater, or a rocking boat, that will be natural parts of how you set up your space. If not, you can make basic items inexpensively or from recycled materials. While sturdiness and attractiveness are important, items you create need not be fancy. It is often better to let children's imaginations add the details. Consider children's home languages as well as English in the signage and print posted in your play area.

Determine the types and numbers of props to include according to the children's experiences, their levels of understanding, and the resources available to you. The principle "less is more" is often a good one to follow when setting up dramatic-play centers. While too few props can limit children's involvement or the roles they can play, too many can be overwhelming and stifle children's creativity. Remember, your goal should be to support their creative expression rather than your own! Initially, providing open-ended, multipurpose materials and including some that are related to the theme will get them started and inspire them to innovate. Add others as your observations of their play dictate.

Be sure to include props that support the various roles associated with the theme to encourage children's social interactions and their cognitive, language, and emotional skills. For example, roles in a restaurant include the cooks, servers, and customers. Roles in a shoe store include salespeople and customers. Clothing and other items that help children step into a particular role make it easier for them to act in character.

You might decide an idea for facilitating engagement will help children plan their play, get started, extend their play, or make connections and build skills and understandings across the curriculum. Strategies are listed as either outside the play frame, where your facilitation takes place outside of the play itself, or as coplayer, where you assume a minor role inside the play scenario and act accordingly. Examples of the kinds of questions you might ask and comments you might make are italicized.

While not listed in this section, there are many excellent children's books to support any dramatic play theme you choose. An Internet search or a trip to your local library will help you find selections you can read with children and use as references to enhance understanding and spark imaginative thinking. See Appendix A for a short list of books to inspire dramatic play.

Also included are suggestions for related experiences to help connect the intellectual dispositions children develop during dramatic play with some of the academic skills that are codified in program and state early learning standards. For example, when encouraged to retell or dictate stories about what they have pretended, children construct short narratives to communicate effectively. When they draw or write about their play, they demonstrate a variety of emergent writing skills.

Airplane

CENTER ARRANGEMENT

Materials:

brads

cardboard

cardboard box

chairs

chart with destinations and departure times

maps

masking or painter's tape

photos of airports, planes, cloud formations, and destinations

scissors

table

Setup:

1. Tape an outline of a plane on the floor.

2. Line up a few chairs inside this outline.

3. Create a simple steering wheel by cutting a circle out of cardboard fastening it with brads to a cardboard box.

4. Set up a table for a ticket counter.

5. Display a chart with destinations and departure times, maps, and/or photos of airports, planes, cloud formations, and destinations, such as a city, a beach, and national parks. Include names of places to which you know children have traveled or where their relatives live.

PROPS

clock

flight-attendant uniforms made from shirts with insignias drawn on

frozen-food trays and plastic cups

ground crew signal wands (red drum sticks, flashlights, or cones made from red cardstock)

headphones for the pilot

pilot hat or shirt with wings drawn on

small carry-on or tote bags

stamp and ink pad for the ticket counter

tickets

travel brochures

FACILITATING ENGAGEMENT

• Add an instrument panel. Draw dials and fasten knobs to a box. Point out what they show—for example, speed, altitude, temperature.

- Provide paper with two columns for recording arrival and departure times.

- Mark passenger chairs with numbers to match the numbers on the boarding passes children get when they check in at the ticket counter.

- During circle time, make a game out of following ground-crew signals.

  - Wave arms up and down for moving straight ahead.

  - Extend left arm and signal with right hand to come ahead for turning right (from children's points of view).

  - Fully extend arms straight out in front for stopping.

- Ask questions such as the following:

  What do you know about airplanes?

  Where would you like to go on an airplane?

  What do you need to pack for the trip you're taking?

  This is Sarah's first plane trip. Can you help her?

Coplayer:

- Ask questions and make comments such as the following:

  I would like a ticket to go to New York City.

  Does my ticket (or boarding pass) show where I should sit?

  I see other airplanes out my window. Where do you think they're going?

How long before we land?

Thank you for bringing me a glass of water.

RELATED EXPERIENCES

- Make a list with the children of what they need to pack for a trip. Post the list and provide these items in the dramatic-play center.

- After reading stories with airplanes in them, encourage the children to draw or paint stories about flying in an airplane. Take dictation as they tell about their artwork.

- Encourage the children to draw on cellophane what they imagine seeing out the window of an airplane. These can be mounted on white paper and displayed in the dramatic-play center.

- Mark off the actual length and wingspread of a jet plane on the playground. How many steps long and wide is it?

- Ask children to make and add up tally marks of the airplanes that fly overhead. Talk with them about the different kinds they see.

- On the playground, have children move like airplanes: warming up, taking off, flying, and landing.

- Encourage them to take turns as members of the ground crew using signal wands.

Bakery

CENTER ARRANGEMENT

Materials:

cardboard box

low bookshelf

markers

photos of bread and other baked items

scissors

shoe boxes (optional)

signs and labels: Bakery/*Panadería*, oven, and so on

small kitchen shelf rack

table

tape

Setup:

1. Provide an oven or make one by cutting a door in a sturdy box, attaching a door handle, and drawing on controls. Place a small kitchen shelf rack inside.

2. Use a low bookshelf as a display rack or create one by taping several shoe boxes on top of each other.

3. Add a worktable.

4. Display photos of bread and other baked items. Be sure to include types associated with a variety of cultures as well as ones with which children are most familiar.

5. Include signs and labels: Bakery/*Panadería*, oven, and so on.

PROPS

aprons

assorted baking pans: bread pan, cookie sheet, muffin tin, and so on

bowls

cash register/money box

empty ingredient containers

hand mixer with cord cut off

measuring spoons and cups

Open/Closed sign

play money

potholders

receipt pad

rolling pin

spoons

timer

tortilla press

white board and dry-erase marker for listing prices

FACILITATING ENGAGEMENT

Outside the play frame:

- During large-group time, guide the children in acting out the steps to make bread or cake.

- Invite family members to share and show how they make a traditional baked item such as muffins, tortillas, pan, naan, or injera.

- Visit a local bakery. Talk with children first about what they want to know. Support each of them in asking or finding out answers to their questions. Take photos to post in the center and use to prompt discussions.

- Ask questions such as the following:

  What special things are you baking this week?

  Mmm. That smells yummy! How did you make it?

  Miguel has one dollar. What can he buy in your bakery?

Coplayer:

- Ask questions and make comments such as the following:

  Use the rolling pin or tortilla press to flatten dough.

  I'm making this nice and thin.

  I need to add the right amount of flour and salt so it will be just right.

  Will you let me know when I need to take my cake out of the oven?

I'd like to buy a loaf of bread to make sandwiches.

These cookies are delicious! Do you also sell birthday cakes?

RELATED EXPERIENCES

- Add playdough and additional tools, such as cookie cutters, a garlic press, plastic knives, craft sticks, or candles.

- Tape plastic sheeting under the worktable. Substitute real bread dough and flour for playdough.

- Help children make signs and price lists for the center.

- Add an assortment of measuring cups and spoons to the sensory table or to sand play equipment.

- Make bread with prepackaged bread dough or follow a recipe to make tortillas.

- Encourage the children to draw, dictate, or write directions for making their favorite baked items.

Bank

CENTER ARRANGEMENT

Materials:

cardboard box or tri-fold board

card stock

contact paper or laminator

marker

masking or duct tape

paper

scissors

shoe box

small calculator

table and chairs

Setup:

1. Set up a table and chairs for the bankers.

2. Make a teller window by cutting a window in a cardboard box or tri-fold board that children can look through. Label it and tape it to the table.

3. Create an ATM. Fasten a small calculator to a shoe box, cut slots for bankcards and cash, and add a sign.

4. Make a pathway or indicate in another way where customers can wait in line.

5. Display signs with the bank's name and banking hours and pictures of currencies.

6. Create an illustrated diagram showing coin and dollar-bill equivalencies for the children's reference: 2 nickels = 1 dime, 4 quarters = 1 dollar bill, and so on.

7. Create pretend credit and bank cards out of card stock. Laminate them to make them sturdier.

PROPS

calendar

clothing for the bankers (jacket, shirt, dress, clip-on tie)

computer keyboard

date stamp and ink pad

deposit and withdrawal slips

Open/Closed sign or materials for making signs

paper and pencils

play money (Laminated photocopies of paper bills are sturdier and more realistic than conventional play money.)

small containers or trays

telephone

wallets and purses for bank customers

FACILITATING ENGAGEMENT

Outside the play frame:

- Visit and tour a neighborhood bank to provide concrete background experiences.

- Talk with children and role-play different jobs in a bank.

- Help children make change according to their levels of understanding.

- Make a chart with each child's name at the top of a column. Show them how to list the amount deposited and withdrawn.

- Ask questions such as the following:

Are you going to be a teller or a customer today?

Erina just earned some money from babysitting. How should she make a deposit into her account?

Coplayer:

- As a bank teller, model sorting coins and making change.

- As a customer, model waiting in line to be helped or to use the ATM machine.

- Ask questions such as the following:

Jamal wrote me a check for two dollars. Can you help me cash it?

I need some coins for the parking meter. May I please have change for this dollar bill?

RELATED EXPERIENCES

- Give children small milk cartons for making and decorating individual piggy banks.

- Ask children to estimate the number of pennies in a jar. Record their estimates and then count the pennies to check.

- Provide dollar-bill-size paper and markers. Encourage the children to make their own currency.

- Give each child a job to earn play money to deposit in an individual container (an account) in the bank. Provide small items in a classroom store that children can purchase with their money. Add a penny interest for each day they leave their money in the bank. Periodically, help them figure the balance.

- Tape a penny, nickel, dime, and quarter inside four bowls. Give children a bowl of coins to sort and count.

- Using either lightweight paper or aluminum foil, have children make crayon rubbings of real coins hot glued onto card stock.

Bath Time

CENTER ARRANGEMENT

Materials:

aluminum foil

bathmat

brass fasteners

cardboard

dish tub

labeled chart or drawing of a child's body

large cardboard box

masking tape

packing peanuts

pegboard, hat rack, or clothes-drying rack

photos of adults bathing babies

plastic cup

scissors

table

tape

Setup:

1. Make a bathtub from a sturdy box big enough for at least two children to sit in. If need be, cut it down so it is about 2 feet in height.

2. Cut out two knobs from cardboard, and label them as hot and cold. Affix the knobs with brass fasteners. Make a faucet by covering a plastic cup with aluminum foil. Attach the faucet to the bathtub with tape.

3. Add packing peanuts to the tub for bubbles.

4. Place a bathmat in front of the bathtub.

5. Use a standing pegboard, hat rack, or clothes-drying rack to hang towels and shower caps.

6. Put a dishtub on a table along with items for washing dolls.

7. Display a labeled chart or drawing of children's bodies and pictures of adults bathing babies.

PROPS

aprons

bath toys

dolls and stuffed animals

empty shampoo, bubble-bath, and baby-powder bottles

powder puff

scrub brush

shower caps

sponges

towels and washcloths

FACILITATING ENGAGEMENT

Outside the play frame:

- Invite a parent with a young baby to demonstrate how to give the baby a bath, or use a doll to show children the process.

- Talk with children about what they need to take a bath.

- Ask questions such as the following:

    Can you make room in the bathtub for Franzi? She's been working in the garden.

    This baby needs a bath. Please make sure he's safe in the bathtub.

Coplayer:

Ask questions such as the following:

Ooh! The water is so cold. I'm turning the hot water knob to make it warmer.

I need to wrap my baby up in a towel so he doesn't get cold. Could you please hand me one?

RELATED EXPERIENCES

- Wash dolls in the water table. Add a little tearless shampoo or bubble bath to the water.

- Make bubble prints. Mix tempera paint in a little water, stir in a few squirts of dish-washing liquid, and use a straw to blow lots of bubbles into it. Gently place paper over the bubbles to make a print.

- Make toy boats. Provide an assortment of small items that will float, such as small wooden blocks or sponges, walnut shells, Styrofoam trays, or three corks with a rubber band around them, and materials for making boats, such as toothpicks, craft sticks, straws, and paper.

Bedtime

CENTER ARRANGEMENT

Materials:

curtain

dark fabric

dark-colored paper

hole punch

nap mats, cushions, camping pads, or inflatable mattress

paper or paint

scissors

tape

Setup:

1. Provide several beds, such as nap mats, cushions, camping pads, or an inflatable mattress.

2. Hang a curtain from the ceiling or arrange furniture to make a bedroom wall.

3. Paint or tape stars and a moon on a large piece of dark fabric. Attach the corners of the fabric to the ceiling to create the night sky.

4. Cover the windows with dark paper punched with small holes for stars.

PROPS

blankets

clock

dolls and stuffed animals

flashlights

pajamas, nightgowns, and slippers

pillows

recorded lullabies

storybooks

washcloths, towels, and plastic cups

FACILITATING ENGAGEMENT

Outside the play frame:

• Talk with children about their bedtime routines.

• Read or tell the children a bedtime story during circle time. Consider adding one or two props related to the story.

• Ask questions such as the following:

What do you do to get ready for bed?

Vanessa isn't sleepy yet. Could you read her a bedtime story or sing her a lullaby?

Coplayer:

- Ask questions such as the following:

  Mateo, would you like me to tuck you in?

  Oh! I forgot to wash my face. Could you please hand me a washcloth?

  It's 8 o'clock. Is it time for us to go to bed?

RELATED EXPERIENCES

- Send a request to families to help children record their bedtimes for one week. Attach a form they can use. Make and display a bar graph with children of their respective bedtimes.

- Plan a pajama day where everyone wears sleepwear to school.

- Darken the room and read a bedtime story by flashlight.

- Make hand shadows in front of a flashlight or overhead-projector light.

- Provide dark paper, light chalk, or pastels for children to create night scenes. Add sticky stars.

- Record children singing lullabies or making soft, soothing musical sounds.

Camping

CENTER ARRANGEMENT

Materials:

blocks

camp stools or beach chairs

cooler

photos of mountains, forests, deserts, and beaches

red and yellow cellophane

small logs, paper-towel rolls, or rolled-up newspaper

tent or bedsheet and rope

wire grate

Setup:

1. Set up a real tent, or drape a sheet over a line stretched horizontally from points on two walls. Alternatively, cut a door in the sheet and use it to cover a table.

2. Build a campfire made from small, smooth logs; paper towel rolls; or rolled-up newspaper. Add red and yellow cellophane for the flames.

3. Place a cooling rack or small wire grate on several blocks surrounding the campfire to make a grill for cooking.

4. Display photos of mountains, forests, deserts, and beaches.

5. Provide a cooler and campstools or beach chairs.

PROPS

backpacks

binoculars (Cut a paper-towel roll in half, and tape the halves together.)

canteen or reusable water bottles

clothing, such as hats, bandanas, and jackets

compass

empty food packages and cans

first-aid kit

flashlights

plastic plates, cups, and utensils

pot or pan

sleeping bags or blankets

sunglasses

trail map

FACILITATING ENGAGEMENT

Outside the play frame:

• Invite a family member or a park ranger to talk about camping and caring for the environment.

- Darken the room, sit around the campfire, and sing songs.

- Take children on an imaginary camping trip during large-group time. Encourage them to suggest what they will do and what equipment they will need.

- Ask questions such as the following:

    Are you camping in a good place to hike? How do you know?

    Can you help Tyrone adjust the straps on his backpack?

    What are you cooking over your campfire?

Coplayer:

- Model reading a trail map or using a compass.

- Ask questions such as the following:

    I think I see a deer through my binoculars. Do you see it?

    We have to be sure not to leave any trash behind when we leave. Do you see any we need to clean up?

    What should we do so we can see after it gets dark?

RELATED EXPERIENCES

- Make a trail map for children to follow on the playground. At each destination on the map, encourage them to collect leaves, twigs, and pebbles that they can use to create nature collages.

- Add props for fishing. (See the Fishing theme on page 127.)

- After looking at features on a simple trail map, provide materials in the art center for children to use to create their own maps.

- Provide a tape or CD of camp songs in the music center.

Celebrations

CENTER ARRANGEMENT

Materials:

large calendar

photos of a variety of personal and cultural celebrations

streamers and other decorations

table and chairs

worktable

Setup:

1. Set up a table and chairs.

2. Add a separate worktable.

3. Drape streamers and/or other culturally related decorations from the ceiling.

4. Display a large calendar and a variety of photos of personal and cultural celebrations.

PROPS

basket of ribbons

camera

crayons or markers

dress-up clothes

empty boxes

gift bags

paper

pitcher

plastic plates, cups, and utensils

tablecloth and napkins

FACILITATING ENGAGEMENT

Outside the play frame:

- Read books about celebrations for special occasions, such as birthdays, weddings, fiestas, or the New Year.

- Talk with children about their own birthday celebrations and other special occasions their families celebrate. Add related props to the center.

- Invite family members to talk with children about their cultural celebrations and to share photos, songs, dances, or other activities.

- Add props for making party foods.

- Ask questions such as the following:

  What special occasion are you celebrating today?

  Can you help Dimitri button his vest?

Coplayer:

- Narrate what you are doing as you pretend to make food associated with an occasion that one or more of the children celebrate.

- Ask questions such as the following:

My sister wants cupcakes for her graduation party so I'm going to make her some. Would you like to help?

Would you pour me another cup of tea, please?

Aailyah, please help me blow out these candles.

RELATED EXPERIENCES

- Provide paper folded in half and art supplies for the children to use to make invitations and greeting cards.

- Make and decorate party hats.

- Whip soap flakes with a little water until the mixture is the consistency of whipped cream. Color small amounts with food coloring. Place this "frosting" in several small ziplock bags. Snip a small corner off each bag to make cake-decorating tubes. Squeeze the frosting onto upside-down recycled food containers and trays.

- In the music center, add tapes or CDs and instruments related to children's family celebrations. A few articles of clothing can also encourage children to dance to the music.

Construction Site

CENTER ARRANGEMENT

Materials:

hat rack or standing pegboard

labeled photos or diagrams of common tools

photos of construction workers, construction projects,
    and building sites

plastic crate or carryall

safety cones or yellow tape

shelves

table

Setup:

1. Set up safety cones or yellow tape to mark the boundaries of the construction zone.

2. Add a plastic crate or carryall for tools.

3. Provide a table for a workbench, shelves to hold hard hats and other materials, and either a hat rack or standing pegboard for hanging work clothes.

4. Display pictures of construction workers, construction projects, and building sites. Include pictures of both female and male construction workers.

5. Post labeled photographs or diagrams of common tools.

PROPS

assorted boxes

blueprints or plans for building structures (You can download these from the Internet.)

bucket

card stock or cardboard

clipboard

crayons

hard hats

paintbrushes and paint rollers

paper

pencils

ruler

safe building-supply scraps and smooth pieces of wood

safety goggles

small sections of PVC pipe and elbow joints

tape measure

tools, such as hammers, screwdrivers, and pliers

work gloves

work shirts or vests

yardstick

FACILITATING ENGAGEMENT

Outside the play frame:

- Visit a nearby construction site to provide background experiences. Take photos.

- Discuss and post photos of the site.

- Encourage children to draw their observations on clipboards during the excursion or afterward while in the art center.

- Post children's drawings of construction in the dramatic-play center.

- Invite a family member who works in construction to tell about his work and show how to use simple tools of the trade. Alternatively, invite the school's maintenance person to stop by and perhaps let children watch a repair in progress.

- Ask questions such as the following:

  I wonder what you can construct from these things. What do you think?

  That looks like a big project and might need more workers.

  Sophia, do you think you could help Jackson with these pliers?

Coplayer:

- Model following a diagram (blueprint) to try to build something.

- Ask questions such as the following:

  This is heavy. Would you please help me move it?

  Wait, I have to put on safety goggles before I use these tools. Would you please hand them to me?

RELATED EXPERIENCES

- Provide small wood scraps, empty paper-towel rolls, and collage materials in the art center so that small groups of children can make a structure together. Once complete, take dictation about its features from each child. Include all the descriptions when it is displayed.

- Place a tree stump on the playground. Provide safety goggles, real hammers, and real nails. Closely supervise children as they pound nails into the stump.

- Post diagrams of construction sites or blueprints of building plans downloaded from the Internet in the art center. Add graph paper and rulers to the art supplies.

- Add old keys and a box of spare nuts, bolts, washers, and other hardware fasteners to the art center for use in assemblages.

- Include a tape or CD with traditional work songs in the music center.

- Line up pipe sections and dowels of different diameters and lengths on a Styrofoam box, strip of foam rubber, or inverted egg carton. Provide rhythm sticks, spoons, pencils, or mallets for children to use to experiment with different tones and pitches.

Fishing

CENTER ARRANGEMENT

Materials:
blue tarp, plastic tablecloth, or sheet
boat or cardboard box or plastic storage bin
Gone Fishing sign
photos of lakes, rivers, oceans, and fish
stools or carpet squares
tape

Setup:

1. Tape a blue tarp, plastic tablecloth, or sheet to the floor.

2. Add a rocking boat, or make a boat from a sturdy box or a two-foot high plastic storage container that at least two children can sit in. Alternatively, tape the outline of a boat on the floor, and place a few stools or carpet squares inside.

3. Display photos of lakes, rivers, oceans, and fish.

4. Add a Gone Fishing sign.

PROPS

empty tackle box

fish shapes of different sizes cut from cardstock or craft foam with paper clips on their mouths

fishing poles (sticks, dowels, or rulers with a cord and magnet tied to each)

life preservers

nets

rain boots

ruler

small bucket

small cooler

sun hats, sunglasses, and jackets

FACILITATING ENGAGEMENT

Outside the play frame:

• Ask the children what they know about fishing.

- Invite a family member who fishes to talk with children about fishing and the equipment that is needed.

- Ask questions such as the following:

  What do you need to take on your fishing trip?

  What will you do if there is a storm?

Coplayer:

- Ask questions such as the following:

  Can you show Vanessa and me how you caught that fish?

  If I keep still, I won't scare the fish and the boat won't capsize!

  Wow! That's a big fish! Let's measure it.

  My fish is too small to eat. I'm going to throw it back into the water.

RELATED EXPERIENCES

- Visit a nearby lake or pond or pet or aquarium store.

- Add fishing poles with opened paper-clip hooks instead of magnets. Make fish from paper-towel rolls cut in half. Cut two slits opposite each other in one end of each roll. Slip a triangle-shaped "tail" into the slits. Punch about ten holes in the roll. Draw on eyes and other fish markings. Trying to hook the fish through the holes adds challenge.

- Fill a child's wading pool with several inches of water. Make fish by drawing on foam packing pieces and/or by cutting shapes from craft foam. Add a paper clip to the mouth end of each fish. Place the fish in the water, and use nets and fishing poles with magnets on one end to catch the fish.

- Purchase several whole fish from the market. Make fish prints by painting them with tempera and pressing paper on top.

- Create a class fish mural by painting a big piece of butcher paper with a mixture of blue paint and shaving cream. When it is dry, children can glue on fish they have drawn and cut out.

- Add fish wands (paint stirrers with fish taped to the top) and streamers to the music center along with a tape or CD of appropriate instrumental music, such as Handel's *Water Music.*

- Put a donated rowboat (stripped of anything hazardous) in a sandy area on the playground.

Grocery Store

CENTER ARRANGEMENT

Materials:

markers

masking or painter's tape

newspaper grocery ads

paper

photos of food products

photos of local grocery stores

shelves

table

Setup:

1. Use a table for a check-out counter.

2. Set up shelves or tables for grocery items.

3. Label store sections: dairy, deli, frozen, meat, produce, canned goods, and cleaning products.

4. Mark the check-out lane with tape on the floor.

5. Display grocery-store ads and photos of food products.

6. Post photos of grocery stores in your areas. Include their names.

PROPS

aprons

assorted bottles, cans, and boxes of grocery-store items (Tip: Stuff empty boxes with newspaper and tape them shut to make them more durable.)

baskets with handles

cash register and/or money box

coupons

egg cartons with plastic eggs

markers for making signs (Open/Closed, Sale)

name tags, such as cashier, bagger, and stocker

notepads and pencils for making grocery lists and receipts

paper or paper plates

plastic fruit and vegetables

play money

receipt pad

reusable cloth shopping bags

scale for weighing produce

stickers for writing prices

wallets and purses for shoppers

FACILITATING ENGAGEMENT

Outside the play frame:

- Talk with children about the sections in a grocery store: produce, dairy, meat, and frozen food.

- Talk with children about the different jobs of the employees: stocker, butcher, cashier, and bagger.

- Visit a local grocery store. Point out different sections and signs. Help children interview store workers about their jobs. Purchase ingredients for making a simple recipe or something for snack like veggies and a dip. Take photos of different sections to post in the dramatic-play center.

- Brainstorm and vote on the name for the class grocery store.

- Ask questions such as the following:

  Hong, the store needs someone to bag groceries. Would you like to help?

I think Samantha is waiting for you tell her how much her groceries cost.

I see you have cake mix in your basket. What are you buying for dinner?

Coplayer:

- Think out loud as you model how to pay for the items in your shopping basket.

  Which of these soups costs less?

  I'm weighing these potatoes. I need one pound for dinner.

  Are you in line to check out? I'll stand behind you.

RELATED EXPERIENCES

- Give each child the same amount of play money to spend in the grocery store. Help them compare what they can buy. Can they buy a well-balanced meal with it?

- Gather food items that begin with each letter of the alphabet. During circle time or with a small group, ask children to choose the item that begins with each letter.

- Weigh real fruit and vegetables, and record their weights on a premade form.

- Show children containers of different sizes for food items, such as milk cartons, canned vegetables, yogurt tubs, and cereal boxes. Have them order them by size. Talk with them about equivalencies (2 half gallons = 1 gallon).

- On a tray, place five or six food items from the same category, such as dairy foods. Add one item from a different category, such as canned goods. Ask children to identify the item that doesn't belong.

- Give children supermarket circulars to cut out coupons or find photos of food to glue onto on a paper plate to make a picture of a nutritious meal. Talk about nutritious foods.

- Use empty food containers for assemblages in the art center or to make sound makers for the music center. Add appropriate art supplies to decorate and personalize creations.

Hair Salon/Barber Shop

CENTER ARRANGEMENT

Materials:
bench

chairs

dry-erase marker

empty paper-towel roll

photos of boys, girls, men, and women of different ethnicities and with different hairstyles

red, white, and blue paint

small whiteboard

table

tape or upright paper-towel holder

nonbreakable floor mirror

Setup:

1. Set up several chairs for customers in front of a table for the stylists/barbers.

2. Use a bench or one or two chairs for the waiting area.

3. Add a nonbreakable floor mirror.

4. Stand a whiteboard on the table. Include a dry-erase marker for writing prices.

5. Make a barber's pole by covering a paper towel roll with white, red, and blue stripes. Tape it to the wall or put it in an upright paper towel holder.

6. Display photos of boys, girls, men and women of different ethnicities and with different hairstyles.

PROPS

appointment book

cash register or money box

clipboard or pad of paper and a pencil for the wait list

clock

combs, brushes, hair picks (If included, sanitized after use.)

container with hair accessories, such as scrunchies, headbands, and hairclips

dish pan for washing hair

dolls with hair to style

empty hair-care product containers, such as shampoo, conditioner, and gel

electric shaver without cord or batteries

foam curlers

hair dryer with cord cut

magazines for the waiting area

old shower nozzle

play money

scissors that don't cut

smocks or capes

telephone

towels

nonbreakable hand mirror

wallets and purses

FACILITATING ENGAGEMENT

Outside the play frame:

- Talk with children about getting their hair cut or going to a hair salon or barber shop. Ask them to demonstrate what the barber or hairstylist did.

- Ask what they would need for their classroom salon. Show and describe props that will be in the dramatic-play center.

- Ask them to brainstorm and then vote on names for the classroom salon. Help them to create a sign.

- Invite a family member or local hairdresser to talk with the children and demonstrate how some items are used.

- Ask questions such as the following:

  What time is your appointment?

  Are you going to shampoo Mateo's hair before you cut it?

Coplayer:

- Be a willing customer, and allow children to style your hair!

- Ask questions such as the following:

  My hair has gotten too long. I need a haircut. Can you do it?

  Can you make my straight hair curly?

  The sign says a shampoo and cut is five dollars, but a haircut is just three dollars. My hair is clean, so I'm just going to have it cut for three dollars.

RELATED EXPERIENCES

- Add a mannequin styling head.

- Add grooming accessories, particularly ones for boys, such as a shaving cup and brush, a razor without a blade, an empty after-shave bottle, and clip-on ties.

- With parents' permission, use gel to sculpt each child's hair. Provide hand mirrors, and encourage the children to make self-portraits in the art center.

- Fingerpaint with shaving cream on a table in the art center. Add craft stick "shavers."

- Provide round or oval paper in different skin tones. Add markers for the children to use to make faces on the paper. Provide different colors of yarn, pompoms, and sandpaper scraps for children to use to make hair.

Hospital

CENTER ARRANGEMENT

Materials:

2 half-inch dowels

baby blanket

bath towel

blanket

heavy-duty stapler or needle and thread (adult only)

human body and growth charts

markers

nap mats, cots, or lawn-chair cushions

old X-rays (or draw some on transparency sheets)

photos of medical personnel

pillow

poster board

sheet or sign marked with a red cross and the word *Hospital*

shelves or stacking bins

small table

standing pegboard or hat rack

wagon

Setup:

1. Set up one or two hospital beds using nap mats, cots, or lawn-chair cushions.

2. Drape a small table with a baby blanket to use as a dolls' hospital bed.

3. Add shelves or stacking bins for props and a standing pegboard or hat rack to hang clothing.

4. Place a blanket and pillow inside a wagon for the ambulance.

5. Make a stretcher by folding the sides of a bath towel over half-inch dowels and sewing or stapling them in place.

6. Use a sheet marked with a red cross to cover a wall or divide your space. You can also post a Hospital sign at the entrance of the dramatic-play center.

7. Add Emergency Room, Doctor Is In, and Waiting Room signage.

8. Post old X-ray films or pretend X-rays made from overhead transparency sheets, human body and growth charts, and images of medical personnel. Be sure to include female doctors and male nurses.

PROPS

blankets

blue shirts for ambulance driver/paramedic

casts made from white athletic socks with the feet cut off

child-friendly items donated by families involved in health care

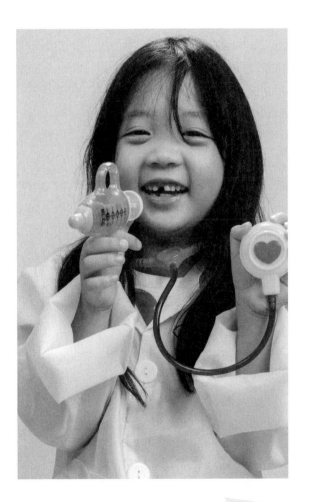

child-size crutches

clipboards with pencils attached and paper for patient charts

computer keyboard

dolls

elastic bandages

empty medicine bottles

latex gloves

medical masks

scarves for slings

shower cap or disposable hair caps

stethoscope (real or toy) or one made by inserting a funnel
   in half a paper-towel roll and taping it securely in place

syringes (toy or real with needles removed)

telephone

thermometers (craft sticks, each to be used only once)

white shirts for hospital personnel

Optional: cotton balls, adhesive bandages, and other
   expendable and single-use supplies

FACILITATING ENGAGEMENT

Outside the play frame:

- Ask children to share what they know about hospitals.
  Add or introduce props based on this discussion.

- Invite a health-care professional to talk with children
  about how she cares for patients.

- Role-play with children what happens when you go to
  the hospital.

- Ask questions and make comments such as the following:

Isabella had an accident and broke her arm. Can you take her to the hospital?

Call 911 for the ambulance!

Coplayer:

- Take turns with children using a stethoscope to listen to each other's hearts.

- Ask questions and make comments such as the following:

My baby is sick. He needs to go to the hospital.

I have a bad cut on my arm. Can you help me?

Can you hear my heart beat?

RELATED EXPERIENCES

- Talk with children about calling 911 in medical emergencies. Help them practice dialing those numbers.

- Add scales (adult and baby) and a height-measurement strip taped to the wall. Measure and record each child's weight and height.

- Discuss why children should take medicine only with adult supervision.

- Make a matching game by downloading a diagram of body parts. Cut it into parts (torso, leg, arm, neck, ear, foot, hand, and finger). Make cards with corresponding labels so that children can match the word to each part. Alternatively, download images of X-rays of body parts, and help children match words to the images.

• Cut a cardboard skeleton into pieces for children to put back together. Label each piece.

Library

CENTER ARRANGEMENT

Materials:

book-display rack

book shelves

crate

floor pillows or a bean-bag chair

index cards

markers

paper

pocket chart

posters with book illustrations or ones from National Library Week

table and chairs

Setup:

1. Set up a table with chairs on one side for the librarians.

2. Label book shelves with sections for different genres: fiction, nonfiction, and poetry.

3. Add a book-display rack to feature particular books.

4. Use a crate as a book bin, and label it with a "Please Return Books Here" sign.

5. Include floor pillows or a bean-bag chair for story hour.

6. Post a pocket chart with children's names on the pockets. Index cards from books they check out can be placed in the pockets.

7. Display signs, such as "Dive into a Book," "Shh, I'm reading," and posters with book illustrations or ones from National Library Week.

PROPS

assorted books with check-out cards made from index cards placed between pages or into pockets made from cut-down envelopes attached to the inside covers

calendar

cardstock and markers for making signs, such as Quiet Please and Check Out

date stamp and ink pad

library cards for each child

magazines

note pad and pencils for making overdue notices

stuffed animals to read to

FACILITATING ENGAGEMENT

Outside the play frame:

- Visit the school library. Focus on check-out and return procedures.

- Invite the school librarian or a family member to read stories to small groups of children.

- Visit a neighborhood library during story hour. Collect application forms for library cards to send home with the children.

- Talk with the children about how to find a book, check it out, and return it.

- Ask questions and make comments such as the following:

  Jamal wants to listen while you read that story.

  Can you help Carlos check out this book?

Coplayer:

- Ask questions and make comments such as the following:

  Where can I find a book about animals?

  I want to check out this book. What day will I need to return it?

RELATED EXPERIENCES

- Ask children to nominate and then vote on their favorite books in each genre.

- Create book jackets for favorite books in the art center.

- Make bookmarks from recycled materials, such as old file folders, fabric scraps glued onto cardstock, paint-chip cards, or painted craft sticks. Alternatively, put a loop of clear packing tape (sticky side out) around each child's wrist. Go on a nature walk so they can collect different kinds of leaves. Then, stick the tape onto card stock cut to measure. Punch a hole in each bookmark for a ribbon or piece of yarn.

• Display music-related books in the music center.

Movie Theater

CENTER ARRANGEMENT

Materials:
chairs or carpet squares
hat rack or standing pegboard with hooks
movie posters
small table
tape or large nonslip rug
white sheet or window shade

Setup:
1. Mark the stage area with tape on the floor or a large nonslip rug. Alternatively, use your furniture to set this space apart from the rest of the center.

2. Place several chairs or line up a row of carpet squares facing the stage for the audience.

3. Set up a small table for the ticket counter.

4. Add a hat rack or standing pegboard with hooks to hang clothing.

5. Hang a white sheet or a window shade in back of the stage area to serve as a screen.

6. Post movie posters.

PROPS

assorted clothing for the actors

cash register or money box

containers for concession snacks

empty raisin or candy boxes stuffed with newspaper and taped shut

jackets for the ticket seller and usher

microphones made from paper-towel rolls cut in half and topped
   with golf or Ping-Pong balls (Stuff the paper-towel roll with
   newspapers, and wrap the microphone with black tape.)

plastic or paper cups

play money

popcorn boxes, possibly with cotton balls or packing peanuts inside

projector made from a shoe box with hinged lid, a half a
   paper-towel roll for the lens, and a plastic plate for the film reel

signage (Open/Closed, Coming Attractions, Ticket Prices) or a
   whiteboard and dry-erase marker for children to make their
   own signs

tickets

FACILITATING ENGAGEMENT

Outside the play frame:

- After rereading or retelling children a favorite story, ask
  what props they would need to make a movie out of it. Use
  their comments to add items to the dramatic-play center.

- Alternatively, talk with children about their favorite
  movies or television shows. Focus on what they like

about the plot and characters. Discuss how each movie has a beginning, a middle, and an end.

- Ask questions and make comments such as the following:

  It looks like they need a ticket-taker. Here's a basket you can put the tickets in.

  I wonder what snacks they sell at this theater.

Coplayer:

- Ask questions and make comments such as the following:

  How much do tickets cost?

  Thank you showing me to my seat.

RELATED EXPERIENCES

- Take dictation from children about their movie script.

- Dim the lights. Shine a flashlight or overhead projector light onto the stage.

- Videotape the children's movie. Play it back to encourage their comments and extend their play.

- Provide poster-size paper for children to work together in the art center to make movie posters and/or advertisements to display in the dramatic-play center.

- Make popcorn with the children, measuring ingredients together. Compare the volume of unpopped kernels with the popped corn.

- Shine a light on the sheet or screen suspended from the ceiling with enough room behind it for several children. Their actions will be projected onto the sheet so that the audience can see their shadows.

- Include a tape or CD of children's songs that children can sing along to and one or more microphones in the music center.

Optical Shop

CENTER ARRANGEMENT

Materials:

chairs

eye charts: one with letters and one with pictures

photos of people wearing glasses

shelf or display rack

table

Setup:

1. Set up a table and chair for the eye doctor.

2. Use a shelf or display rack for props and eyeglasses.

3. Add one or two chairs for patients who are getting their eyes examined.

4. Post eye charts, one with letters and one with pictures.

5. Display pictures of a variety of people wearing glasses.

PROPS

appointment book

cash register or money box

children's sunglasses

empty contact-lens boxes

eye cover made by taping a black cardboard circle to a tongue
   depressor or craft stick

eye droppers

eye-viewing equipment, such as a View-Master or binoculars

eyeglass cases

eyeglasses without lenses or dollar-store sunglasses with the lenses
   removed

magnifying glass

pad of paper and pencil for writing prescriptions and receipts

play money and credit cards

nonbreakable mirrors

white shirts or smocks for the eye doctor and assistants

FACILITATING ENGAGEMENT

Outside the play frame:

- Talk with children about why people wear corrective lenses, both eyeglasses and contact lenses.

- Ask children what they know about glasses and contact lenses. You may have "experts" in your class who wear glasses.

- Invite a family member who works in optometry to visit the class and tell children about her work. Alternatively, visit an optometrist's office to interview the optometrist and assistant and view equipment and eyeglasses on display.

- Ask questions and make comments such as the following:

Here's a chair for you to sit in while you try on glasses.

Which frames do you like best? Which one costs more?

Coplayer:

- Ask questions and make comments such as the following:

It's time to have my eyes checked. When is the next appointment for a vision screening?

I need glasses to read this book. They make the words bigger so it's easier for me to see them.

RELATED EXPERIENCES

- Talk with children about eye protection and care, such as wearing safety glasses and having regular vision screening.

- Ask children to record how many people they see in one day who wear regular glasses and sunglasses.

- Create eyeglasses for each child from pipe cleaners, or create binoculars by taping two halves of a paper-towel roll together.

- Have children draw portraits of themselves wearing glasses.

- Add eye masks to the music center to encourage children's focus on sounds.

Post Office

CENTER ARRANGEMENT

Materials:

empty cereal or shoe boxes or segmented bottle cartons

large cardboard box

markers

paper

postal rate chart

poster of real stamps

scissors

tables

tape

trays or flat boxes

Optional: blue spray paint and free labels from the post office

Setup:

1. Set up a table for the post-office workers.

2. Place mailboxes marked with children's names on top of another table. These can be made from segmented bottle cartons or by taping stacked cereal or shoe boxes together.

3. Add trays or flat boxes marked *Incoming Mail* and *Outgoing Mail*, as well as several flat containers to help organize stamps, labels, paper, envelopes, and office supplies.

4. Create a freestanding mailbox from a sturdy cardboard box. Cut a slot in the top where the children can "mail" their letters. Cut a drop-down door at the bottom for

removing the mail. Optionally, spray paint it blue and tape on free labels from your local post office.

5. Display a postal rate chart and a chart of real stamps.

PROPS

boxes of different sizes

cash register or money box

cloth tote bags for use as letter-carrier bags

date stamp and stamp pad

index cards (for postcards)

junk mail

paper and envelopes

pencils and markers

play money

receipt pad

scale to weigh small packages

shirts for postal workers

sticky labels or junk mail stamps or cancelled stamps and glue stick

wallets and purses

Optional: U.S. Postal Service Priority Mail boxes (free from the post office) stuffed with newspaper or heavier weighted materials and taped closed

FACILITATING ENGAGEMENT

Outside the play frame:

• Visit the local post office or meet the mail carrier when she delivers the mail.

- Ask a postal clerk for any items that are available free to teachers. Talk with children about the information on these materials.

- Take a walk in the neighborhood to look at mailboxes on homes and businesses. Alternatively, take photos of various mailboxes to post in the dramatic-play center.

- Have each child write or draw messages to a family member. Mail these letters at the nearest mailbox or give them to the mail carrier in the office.

- Project images of different kinds of stamps onto a whiteboard or screen. Discuss the artwork and information on the stamps.

- Ask questions and make comments such as the following:

Can you help Jeremy find Hong's mailbox?

I see you're delivering letters today. Your friends will be happy to receive some mail.

Is there someone special you would like to mail a letter to?

Coplayer:
- Think out loud as you model how to weigh a package and use the postal-rate chart to find how much it will cost to mail it.

I'd like to buy a stamp to mail this letter. How much does it cost?

When do you think my package will arrive?

RELATED EXPERIENCES

- Ask children to design their own stamps. Trim the edges with pinking shears.

- Add packing peanuts and squares of bubble wrap to collage materials in the art center.

- Provide junk mail for the children to sort into different bins: magazines, letters, advertisements, and so on.

- Help children practice learning and/or writing their names and addresses.

Restaurant

CENTER ARRANGEMENT

Materials:

low bookshelf

markers

menu with pictures of foods

paper

play cupboard unit or large cardboard box

sink-stove play unit or large cardboard box

small table

table and chairs

Setup:

1. Arrange kitchen furniture (sink-stove unit and cupboard) if you have them, or make this equipment from sturdy boxes.

2. Set up a table and chairs for customers.

3. Make space on a counter or one end of a low bookshelf for the servers' props.

4. Add a small table for the cashier.

5. Add Open/Closed signs and, once children have decided on it, the restaurant's name.

6. Post a menu with pictures of foods children suggest and their prices.

PROPS

aprons

assorted clothing, such as shirts, blouses, dresses, shoes, scarves, and so on

bowls

cash register or money box

cloth napkins

cooking utensils

dish pan for washing dishes

empty food cans and boxes

measuring cups and spoons

menus

pads and pencils for servers and cashier

pans

pencils

pitcher

plastic plates, utensils, and cups

play money and credit cards

pot holders

purses and wallets

salt and pepper shakers

tablecloth or place mats

* Note: Including play food limits what can be served in the restaurant and dampens children's imaginations.

FACILITATING ENGAGEMENT

Outside the play frame:

- Tour the school cafeteria or a nearby restaurant. Point out different jobs people do. If possible, interview employees.

- After discussing with children their experiences eating at a restaurant, add related props. This discussion may determine the type of dramatic-play restaurant you create.

- Ask children to brainstorm and then vote on the name for their restaurant. Help them make a sign.

- Demonstrate how to set a table for their restaurant, for example with knives, forks, and spoons; chopsticks and rice bowls; or teacups and saucers.

- Ask questions and make comments such as the following:

That soup looks delicious. Are you serving anything else with it?

The dirty dishes are piling up. I think this restaurant needs someone to wash dishes. Would you like to help?

It doesn't look like there are enough place settings for everyone.

Coplayer:

- Model looking at a menu and ordering.

  What you do you recommend?

  Can you please take my order?

  How much does this cost?

RELATED EXPERIENCES

- Show children examples of different kinds of menus. Provide folded paper and markers for them to make their own menus with their favorite foods.

- Include playdough that children can use to make food items.

- Prepare a snack with children that can be served in the restaurant.

- Alternatively, create a food truck by draping a heavy silver tarp with a window cut out over a table or by cutting out the top and making a window in the side of a large refrigerator box. Leave the bottom side connected to make a shelf, and add brackets to hold up the shelf. When set up outside, children can drive up to the window on wheeled toys.

Shoe Store

CENTER ARRANGEMENT

Materials:

2 tables

cardboard or an adult-size insole

chairs

labeled diagram of a shoe

low bookshelf

markers

paper

photos of people wearing different kinds of shoes

stool or footrest

tape

Setup:

1. Line up several chairs.

2. Provide a low bookshelf to hold shoes and other items.

3. Add two tables, one for the sales counter and another for cleaning shoes.

4. Include a low stool or footrest for customers to use as they try on shoes.

5. Post signs, such as the store name, Open/Closed, and Sale.

6. Display pictures of people wearing different kinds of shoes, such as ballet dancers, construction workers, cowboys and cowgirls, nurses, and so on.

7. Create a diagram of one or more shoes. Label their parts.

8. Create a shoe-size measurer from cardboard or from an adult insole marked with children's shoe sizes and taped on the floor.

PROPS

cash register or money box

cleaning materials, such as a brush, cloth, sponge, and empty shoe-polish can

jackets for sales people

paper and pencils to record shoe sizes

play money and credit cards

purses and wallets

receipt pad

ruler to measure feet

shoe boxes

shoe catalogues

shoe horns

shoe trees

socks

telephone

nonbreakable floor mirror

variety of shoes, especially children's shoes such as athletic shoes, boots, dress shoes, moccasins, sandals, slippers, and so on

FACILITATING ENGAGEMENT

Outside the play frame:

• Talk with children about different kinds of shoes, the ways shoes fasten, and the materials out of which they can be made.

- Visit a shoe store or shoe repair shop.

- Ask children to point to different parts of the shoes they are wearing, such as the toe, sole, tongue, eyelet, strap, and so on.

- Ask questions and make comments such as the following:

  Can you help Jesse fasten his shoes?

  I think Maya may be interested in some shoes.

Coplayer:

- Ask questions and make comments such as the following:

  Would you please measure my foot and tell me whether these shoes will fit?

  How much do these shoes cost?

RELATED EXPERIENCES

- Measure each child's shoe size. Graph the results.

- Take a neighborhood walk to look for and count different types of shoes.

- Provide collage materials and card-stock shapes of feet and ankles in profile on which children can create their own shoes.

Veterinarian Clinic

CENTER ARRANGEMENT

Materials:

assortment of boxes, crates, laundry baskets,
   or animal carriers

diagram with labeled parts of a dog or other pet

marker

paper

photos or posters of pets

tables and chairs

tape

X-rays of pets

Setup:

1. Set up a table or two and several chairs for the waiting area.

2. Provide an assortment of boxes, crates, laundry baskets, or animal carriers for pet cages.

3. Display photos or posters of pets.

4. Post a diagram with labeled parts of a dog or other pet.

5. Post a Veterinary (or Pet) Clinic sign and an illustrated list of prices for checkups for different kinds of pets. Alternatively, provide materials for children to make these signs.

6. Display X-rays of pets downloaded from the Internet, obtained from a veterinary clinic, or created by drawing on overhead transparency sheets.

PROPS

appointment book

bandages (lengths of gauze or elastic bandages are better than consumable adhesive bandages)

cash register or money box

clipboard with paper (medical chart)

collar and leash

dish pan for bathing pets

empty medicine bottles

empty pet-food cans

fabric squares and clothespins for children to pretend to be the pets

food and water bowls

play money

receipt pad

rubber gloves

scale

splints made from tongue depressors

stethoscope

stuffed animals

syringes, either toy or real with needles removed

telephone

veterinarian coat (white dress shirt cut down to size) and veterinary assistant smock

FACILITATING ENGAGEMENT

Outside the play frame:

• Ask children to tell about their pets, how they care for them, and what they do when they're sick.

- Arrange for a veterinarian or veterinary assistant to visit class and talk with children about the work they do and the animals for whom they care.

- Using a stuffed animal, talk children through the steps of taking a pet to see a veterinarian: making an appointment, putting the animal in a pet carrier, driving to the clinic, checking in, waiting while the vet and assistant examine and treat the pet, paying for their services, and then driving home.

- Ask questions and make comments such as the following:

  What can your assistant do to help you examine that dog?

  It looks like this bunny isn't feeling well. What do you think you should do?

Coplayer:
- Ask questions and make comments such as the following:

  My kitten has a sore paw.

  I'd like to make an appointment. It's time for my dog's rabies shot.

RELATED EXPERIENCES

- Encourage children to draw and "write" about their pets, either real or imagined. Take dictation. Their pictures can be bound into a class book.

- Provide fabric and fake-fur scraps, feathers, yarn, and other collage materials for children to make pets in the art center.

- Adopt a pet. Fish, reptiles, parakeets, or small mammals such as hamsters, guinea pigs, or fancy rats make good classroom pets. Encourage children to participate in caring for it. Pets provide many valuable learning opportunities.

- Ask children to sort pictures of different kinds of pets into categories.

- Add a tape or CD of songs about animals for children to listen to in the music center.

Wash Day

CENTER ARRANGEMENT

Materials:

2 large cardboard boxes

3–4 laundry baskets

basket or bowl

clothes-drying rack or clothesline

ironing board

marker

old knobs and dials (optional)

paper

table

tape

Setup:

1. Create a washer and dryer from large sturdy boxes with dropdown doors cut into the sides. Draw or glue on knobs and dials. Alternatively, cut a circle out of each

of the tops that is slightly smaller than a round laundry basket or plastic bowl. Set the basket or bowl inside the hole and tape on a separate lid.

2. Set up a table for sorting and folding clothes.

3. Add several baskets marked with signs: Light, Dark, Clean, and Dirty.

4. Provide a clothes-drying rack or clothesline.

5. Include an ironing board if possible.

6. Post signage such as Laundromat/*Lavandería*.

PROPS

assorted child-sized clothing, doll clothes, and socks

cloth diapers or small towels that are easy to fold

clothespins

empty detergent containers

hangers

iron, either toy or a lightweight real one with cord removed

rubber gloves

scrub brushes

FACILITATING ENGAGEMENT

Outside the play frame:

- Visit a self-service laundry. Notice the washing machines, dryers, and detergent dispensers.

- Talk with the children about the process of washing clothes.

- Post a list of illustrated steps for washing clothes:

  - Sort clothes by color.

  - Set the temperature of the water.

  - Pour soap into washing machine.

  - Add clothes.

- Ask questions and make comments such as the following:

  Are you washing light clothes or dark clothes?

  Manny needs help folding clothes.

Coplayer:

- Ask questions and make comments such as the following:

These clothes are so dirty. I'm putting them in the washing machine and setting the temperature to warm.

Can you help me find the mate to this sock?

RELATED EXPERIENCES

- Add play quarters and a collection box for coins or coin slots in the washer and dryer.

- Set up a drying rack or short clothesline on the playground. Let children use tearless shampoo to wash small articles of clothing in a water table or dishpan and hang the clothes to dry.

- Add a washboard instrument to the music center.

- Extend the theme by providing house-cleaning props, such as a bucket, sponges, child-size broom and mop, feather duster, empty spray bottles, and cleaning rags.

CHAPTER

5

Ideas for
Art Experiences

As with dramatic play, children's artistic expressions are rooted in their own experiences and the ways they are making sense of them. Any activities you provide should be child initiated and directed so that what each child does and how he does it is unique and personally meaningful. The adage "It's the process, not the product, that's important," should be foremost in your mind. Children's artwork does not have to look like anything in particular, although it may. The main thing is that what they do and how they do it is meaningful to them. A child who is presented with vibrant red, yellow, and blue paint may produce a solidly covered, muddy-brown sheet of paper. But in the process of creating it, he may have used individual colors to make rainbow-like arcs, added swirls that looked to him like a bowl of ice cream, noticed how the paint dripped to make his ice cream melt, added horizontal lines to stop the drips, and focused on how the colors changed with each brush stroke. He was likely thoroughly engrossed, fascinated by what he could make the paint do, and unconcerned that his finished art wasn't tacked to the bulletin board.

Art activities that are open ended and process oriented, rather than planned for children to produce a specific product, encourage them to explore materials and tools and experiment with what they can do with them. They are able to plan, predict, and problem solve instead of depending on the teacher to do that for them. Each of their creations is different; no two look alike. And because there are no teacher-created samples or step-by-step instructions to follow, children can freely express themselves and feel successful. Children who are expected to follow specific directions or patterns can feel frustrated and inadequate when their finished product does not look like the sample. If you have ever heard a child say, "I can't do it. You do it for me," you have witnessed the upshot of that sense of inadequacy. Conversely, open-ended art projects motivate, empower, and help children to feel confident and capable.

Hands-on art can be messy. If you did not do messy art projects yourself as a child, you may initially be uncomfortable with these processes. You may also need to talk with parents about their benefits (as well as encourage them not to send children to school in their best clothes). But after you witness children's engagement and delight in creative self-expression, I hope you will be convinced that potential messes are worth any extra effort on your part. Anticipating how children may use art supplies will help you plan for easier cleanup. Children will also benefit from sharing responsibility for taking care of their art center: they can gather newspapers from the floor, stack trays, or wipe down tables.

STIMULATING CREATIVE EXPRESSION THROUGH ART

While the arrangement of the art center and the materials you provide are primary considerations in supporting creative expression, you can pave the way through your interactions with children. Here are some tips for doing so.

- **Help children recall past experiences and what they know how to do.** Talk with them about what they have done and where they have been. Look at photographs together to encourage conversations.

- **Share great artists' work.** Show children reproductions of great works of art. Help them notice details. Ask questions about what they see, how it makes them feel, what they like best, and how they think the artist created it. Instead of posting cute premade, school-supply-store illustrations, reprints of artists' creations are much more likely to inspire children's experimentation with artistic media and self-expression. Share your own appreciation for different types and styles of art: painting, sculpture, mosaic, realistic, impressionistic, and abstract.

- **Make a special place to display beautiful objects.** A few interesting items on a shelf can arouse curiosity and inspire close observation. Objects might include a shiny seashell, a blooming orchid, folk-art sculpture, an animal figurine, a cornhusk doll, a Chinese cloisonné box, a Central American *mola,* or a piece of kente cloth from Ghana.

- **Use literature.** Motivate children's learning and artistic expression through books. The illustrations in children's picture books vividly portray aspects of the content and are works of art in themselves. Talk with children about the styles and uses of different art elements such as shape, form, color, texture, and line. Many books are specifically about the creative arts. Some of them are listed in Appendix A. They will help you start conversations with children about the kinds of creative expression presented in each.

Make sure books with artful illustrations are accessible at all times.

- **Introduce tools and demonstrate techniques.** Show children how to use new tools and materials. Model techniques, but only as far as children need to get started. For example, if you have supplied corncobs as printing tools, demonstrate how to roll the sides of a cob in a paint tray before rolling it on paper. Expect the children to explore and experiment with tools and materials. They need time to figure out the approaches and techniques that work best for them.

- **Ask open-ended questions.** Help children think critically about the process of creating their art. Ask questions such as, "How does your clay feel?" "Since you've decided to make a house, what materials will you need?" and "What could you use to make the lights on your car?" Ask them about the decisions they made in planning and creating their artwork to help them recognize their thinking and abilities to represent themselves.

  Ask questions such as, "What can you tell me about this picture?" "How did you get that idea?" "How did you make all those pieces stick together?" and "What did you like best about making this?"

- **Give responsive feedback.** What you say and do in response to children's creative efforts matters! An off-handed comment or thoughtless remark can shape children's beliefs in their own abilities and creativity. Blanket statements such as "good job" or judgmental ones such as, "I like . . .," can make children do things just to please adults. If a child asks, "Do you like it?" ask her whether or not she likes or is happy with what she did. Instead of generic praise or conveying your own preferences, offer encouragement by commenting on effort or artistic elements such as color, texture, shape, or pattern in children's creations. This helps them focus on what they have done and how they did it. It also tells them you value their individual thinking and creative efforts. For example:

I see red, yellow, and green all over your paper.

Your sculpture feels so smooth. You worked hard to get all the lumps out of it.

I notice you piled four little playdough balls on top of each other.

You combined so many different materials in your collage.

Your clay cat is thick and solid, so it stands on its own.

You made an interesting design by placing buttons and seeds all around these shapes.

I see lots of swirls on your painting. Can you tell me about them?

Encourage them to go further. When a child indicates he is finished, ask if he needs more paper or paint or if he would like to make something else.

ACTIVITIES AND MATERIALS

Drawing

Making marks or drawing is usually a child's first form of artistic expression in the visual arts. It comes naturally because it is so basic, requiring only a simple tool such as a crayon or even just a finger. While furnishing blank paper and markers is common in early childhood classrooms, there are many other pos-

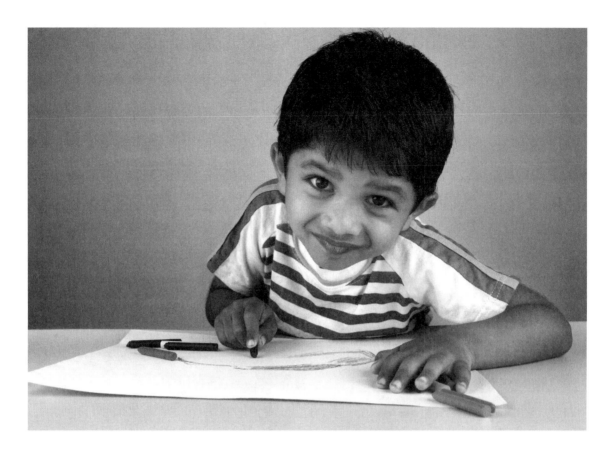

sibilities to inspire and extend children's natural inclination to express themselves creatively through drawing.

- Drawing in sand: Line a baking sheet with a piece of dark paper, and evenly cover it with about half an inch of sand. Children can draw with their fingers. To erase their drawings, gently shake the pan to redistribute the sand.

- Window drawings: Cover a window with window wax. After it is dry, children can draw on the window with their fingers.

- Chalk drawing on wet paper: Dampen construction paper by painting it with water. Provide chalk for children to use. They can also dip pieces of chalk in water to make brighter colors. Alternatively, paint the paper with liquid starch so that the chalk marks will be less blurry.

- Paper-towel pictures: Give children water-based markers to draw on sheets of white paper towel. When their pictures are finished, they can spray their towels with water to mix and blend the colors.

- Crayon resist: Provide crayons, paper, and either watercolor or tempera paint. Children draw a design with the crayons and then paint over it. The paint will coat the paper but not the wax of the crayons. Alternatively, they can draw with glue or paste and, after it is dry, apply paint on top.

- Jump-start drawings: Provide paper you have changed in some way. For example: glue a paper shape of contrasting color on the paper; cut a round, triangular, square, or amorphous hole in the paper, or use a paper punch to punch holes in the paper. These changes further encourage children's creative drawings.

- Picture-frame drawings: Predraw picture frames onto a chalkboard or dry-erase board so children can draw inside of them. If your chalkboard or dry-erase board is big enough, several children can work together on the same drawing.

- Musical drawings: Play instrumental music with different tempos and moods to inspire children to draw what they hear or how the music makes them feel.

- Response drawings: Write a caption on top of the paper to prompt creative thinking. For example:

  - What I wish for

  - An imaginary playground

  - My favorite things

  - I can see (hear, feel, smell, taste)

- Alternatively, predraw the sides and roof of a house on a large sheet of paper or chalkboard so that several children can simultaneously draw their responses to the question, "What's inside this house?" Read a brief story to the children without showing them the pictures to inspire them to draw their own illustrations.

Painting

Children are drawn to paint in all its forms because of its tactile nature and many possible uses. It can be squeezed, spread, brushed, dripped, splattered, and sprayed. It can be smeared or used to make delicate brush strokes. Different kinds of paint and a variety of tools motivate children to experiment and express themselves in many ways.

- Fingerpaintings: Pour one or more puddles of fingerpaint directly onto a smooth surface such as a large sheet of fingerpaint paper, a cookie sheet, a plastic tablecloth

taped securely in place, or the tabletop itself. Once children have spread the paint around and explored its texture with their hands, provide tools such as forks, plastic knives, combs, corks, and foam hair curlers. Let children combine fingerpaint with shaving cream directly on a tabletop. It washes off hands and out of clothing easily and simultaneously cleans the table.

• Easel paintings: Set up one or more easels in the art center. Easels accommodate large paper and children's big brush strokes. They are the perfect height for young children. The trays keep paints and brushes within reach and secure. Liquid or powdered tempera mixed with water are common easel paints because of their viscosity, but other types of materials such as pastels or crayons or even combinations of different media also work well.

- Watercolor paintings: Provide watercolor paints, which are sold in dry pan sets and as liquids. You can also make them using a few basic kitchen ingredients and food coloring (see Appendix B). They make color mixing easy, and they also work well for crayon-resist projects. Special watercolor paper absorbs and distributes watercolor paints well, but it is expensive. Other types of paper can be used for everyday projects with watercolor paper saved for special ones.

- Stained glass windows: Cut easel paper to fit a window or windowpane. The children can use crayons or oil pastels to make designs on their papers before painting over them with liquid watercolors. The light will shine though the watercolor paint when papers are taped to the window.

- Black-line watercolors: Give children permanent black markers to draw shapes, designs, or pictures on paper before completing their pictures with watercolor paint.

- Foam paintings: This thick paint has the consistency of shaving cream (see recipe in Appendix B). Let children paint it onto sturdy paper or cardboard or squeeze it through a ziplock bag. Some dried bits of paint may not permanently stick, but the texture of this paint will encourage experimentation.

- Drip paintings: Put several colors of liquid watercolors in the easel's tray. Give children eyedroppers or pipettes to use to drip paint onto their papers. Encourage pairs of children to do this together.

- Dropper paintings: In small (baby-food size) jars, mix several colors of food coloring with a small amount of water. Provide eyedroppers for children to drip paint onto coffee filters, paper towels, or white felt. The colors will spread through these porous materials making interesting abstract paintings.

- Paper-towel paintings: Let the children draw with washable markers on paper towels and then wet their drawings by lightly painting or dropping water onto them.

- Self-portraits: Copy a photo of a headshot of each child. Glue it at the top of a large sheet of paper. Children paint the rest of their bodies. As an option, they can paint their hands to add their actual handprints to their portraits.

- Scrape paintings: Put several colors of tempera paint into twist-top or plastic catsup bottles. Encourage children to drizzle small amounts of paint onto their papers and then blend the colors by scraping with expired credit cards or similarly sized pieces of cardboard.

- Splatter paintings: Thoroughly cover the painting area with newspaper or plastic drop cloths. Give children small paintbrushes to dip into washable tempera or liquid watercolors so they can fling the paint onto the paper. The paint can also be more gently flicked by tapping the brush. This is a good outdoor art project!

- Condensed-milk paintings: Mix food coloring with several tablespoons of condensed milk in an ice cube tray or in small jars. Give children small brushes to paint this thick, nontoxic paint mixture onto paper or even onto sugar cookies.

- Straw-blown paintings: Give children eyedroppers and straws. Let them drop liquid watercolors onto papers placed in individual trays and then blow through straws to make the paint move and dance across their papers. Have several different kinds of straws on hand so the children can test the effects each makes. (If you cut a small hole near the top of each straw, children will not be able to suck up any paint.)

- Marble or ball paintings: Place paper in the bottom of a box that children can easily hold. Let children squeeze tempera paint from twist-top or catsup bottles onto the paper. Add several marbles. As children tilt their boxes back and forth, the marbles will roll through the paint creating interesting effects. If they have trouble keeping the marbles in the box, wrap the box in plastic wrap so they can still see inside. Taking turns with the same box results in a group painting. Alternatively, pair children: they can hold opposite sides of a bigger box and use marbles, Ping-Pong, or tennis balls to create their paintings.

- Snow paintings: Make snow paint following the recipe in Appendix B. Children can apply this thick and puffy paint onto colored construction paper. The shapes they make will remain after their paintings are dry.

- Mixed-media panels: Provide canvas boards or canvas panels. Set out different thicknesses of paint over a series of days, starting with watercolors and progressing to thick tempera or fingerpaint. Children can apply as much paint as they want on the same panel. If paint layers become especially thick, help them make a print of their painting by pressing a clean sheet of paper on the canvas before continuing the process.

Printmaking

Printmaking allows children to experience cause and effect firsthand as they experiment with different tools and techniques to transfer images onto paper. Basic printing techniques involve dipping three-dimensional objects (the printing tools) into trays or plates of tempera or acrylic paint before pressing them onto paper. Shallow layers of paint work best. Sometimes it is easier to brush paint onto the printing object itself or to apply paint to it with a small paint roller or brayer. Whenever there is an excess amount of paint left on the paper, it can be absorbed by pressing a paper towel over it. If the resulting prints are too blurry, line the tray or plate with felt and soak it with paint. This creates a makeshift stamp pad that will produce sharper prints.

Printing tools to try:

berry baskets

cardboard rolls

cookie cutters

corncobs

dish scrubbers

feathers

flowers with stems long
   enough to be used as handles

kitchen tools, such as a potato masher,
   fork, and spatula

natural items, such as pinecones, seed
   pods, and shells

shoe insoles

thread spools

toy vehicles

wooden blocks

- Bubble prints: Mix tempera paint powder into bubble solution. (See Appendix B for the recipe.) If possible, make several colors. Pour a little of the mixture into a shallow tray or paper plate. Give children straws to blow bubbles in the mixtures. Once a plate is filled with bubbles, they can gently touch paper to the bubbles to make prints. Repeating this process with different colors will result in overlapping bubble shapes in combined colors.

- Bubble-wrap prints: Cut squares of bubble wrap. Pour several colors of paint into paper plates. Children can press the bubble wrap into the paint and then onto their papers.

  Alternatively, wrap children's feet in bubble wrap. Pour several colors of paint into baking pans bigger than their feet, and spread a long sheet from a roll of easel paper on the floor. Let children dip their feet into one color of paint and then walk on the paper to make prints. Overlapping prints of different colors result in a group creation.

- Cork-stamp art: Make cork stamps for children to use. Either glue buttons or shapes cut from shoe insoles or Styrofoam trays onto the bottoms of wine corks. Or wrap three, five, or seven corks together with rubber bands. The resulting prints of bundled corks will resemble flowers.

- Geometric prints: Give children paper cups of various sizes, small square and rectangular boxes, and any packaging materials that have geometric shapes to use to make prints.

- Leaf prints: Encourage children to collect and arrange interesting-shaped leaves on paper. Next, they dip brayers or foam paint rollers in paint before rolling them over the leaves. Show them how to carefully remove the leaves so that the outlines of the leaves appear.

  Alternatively, they can roll paint over the leaves themselves before carefully setting them paint-side down on paper. Show them how to press another sheet of paper on top or use a brayer to roll over the leaves to make their prints.

- Sponge prints: Cut sponges into various shapes. Pinch the center of each sponge with a clothespin to make a handle if the sponge is too thin to easily hold. Encourage children to try printing with both dry sponges and sponges moistened first with water.

- String prints: Provide six- to twelve-inch lengths of string or yarn for children to dip into tempera before dragging the strings across their papers. Alternatively, fold the paper in half. Children can arrange dipped strings on one half of their papers before folding the other half over it to make symmetrical prints.

Rubbings

Rubbings of various objects are simply made by laying a thin piece of paper on top of an object and rubbing over it with the side of a crayon. To help children keep their objects in place, tape their papers to the table or tray first. If leaves or coins are used, the veins of the leaves and the raised parts of the coins will stand out. Give children paper and crayons to take outside to encourage them to look for and make rubbings of objects with different textures. Rubbings can also be painted with watercolors. The wax from the crayons will resist the paint. Provide inkpads for children to make thumb and finger prints on paper. They can complete their prints by drawing on them with thin, felt-tipped markers.

Modeling

Children delight in using flexible modeling materials. Dough and clay beg to be squeezed, patted, poked, rolled, and molded into different shapes. The consistencies of these materials encourage exploration, problem solving, and different forms of self-expression. Adding modeling tools and materials further inspires children's creativity. There is also something soothing and absorbing about playing with these tactile materials. I challenge you to keep your own hands off of them!

Recipes for several kinds of modeling materials can be found in Appendix B. Whenever practical, let children help mix the dough. Some types of dough and clay are more suitable for hardened creations than others. Other types can be reused if kept in airtight containers and refrigerated. A variety of both hardening and nonhardening modeling materials are available through school supply or

craft stores. Choose ones that best fit the children, your purposes, and your budget. Clay boards made from Masonite or linoleum squares will help define each child's work space and make it easier to move artwork to a drying rack.

- Dough and clay additions: Make a modeling toolbox. Possibilities include cookie cutters, plastic utensils, potato masher, roller cutter, rolling pins, and scissors. Add assorted birthday candles, bottle caps, buttons, cardboard tubes, craft sticks, cut straws, feathers, golf tees, wiggly eyes, pipe cleaners, small cars with big tires, small plastic animals, and shells and other natural items. Set out combinations of these materials, for example: bottle caps and straws; pipe cleaners, buttons, and wiggly eyes; or different shells.

- Clay beads: Follow one of the recipes in Appendix B to make paintable clay dough. Show children how to roll a gumdrop- to marshmallow-size piece of dough into a ball. Help them poke a hole through each ball with a chopstick or straw. Once their beads are dry, children can paint them. They are now ready to be strung on shoelaces or lengths of plastic lacing. To supplement the clay beads, provide one-inch pieces of drinking straws so children can make longer strings.

- Papier-mâché sculptures: Choose a form for the sculptures. Bottles, wadded newspaper, small boxes, or paper-towel rolls work well. Help children tape combinations of materials together to make forms. Show them how to put papier-mâché over their forms. Dip half- to one-inch strips of newspaper into a bowl filled with the papier-mâché mixture. (See Appendix B for recipe.) Squeeze out the excess liquid and lay the strips over the base. Smooth the strips into place. Overlap strips and build up layers as needed. Smooth with hands until all the bubbles have been removed. Once children's sculptures are finished, put the sculptures on wax paper and set them aside to dry completely. Let the children paint their sculptures with tempera. Spray finished pieces with hairspray to help seal the paint. Note: Spray the sculptures in a well-ventilated area away from the children.

Collages and Mosaics

Collage and mosaic projects help children make connections as they select and arrange materials to express themselves. They might choose similar or contrasting materials, shapes, and textures. They might plan to create something representational or something abstract, or they may simply explore possibilities as they thoughtfully arrange items. A number of backgrounds are suitable for collages and mosaics: paper, cardboard, box lids, meat trays, paper plates, or even fabric stapled to a rigid base. Whether children use paste or glue depends on the textures and weights of the collage materials as well as on their experience. Paste is often easier for younger, less experienced children to use.

Materials with contrasting colors, shapes, and textures work well in collages and mosaics. This is a good way to use those bits and pieces left over from other projects. Possible items include:

aluminum foil

beads

bottle caps

buttons

cardboard pieces

colored tape

cotton balls

fabric scraps

feathers

jigsaw puzzle pieces

paper scraps such as gift wrap, greeting cards, junk mail, magazines, newspapers, paint chips, and wallpaper samples

pipe cleaners

playing cards

natural materials, such as dried flowers, pebbles, pinecones, seeds, and shells

nuts and bolts

office supplies, such as labels, paper clips, corks, and pen parts

sequins

sewing notions, such as lace, ribbon, and rickrack

small ceramic tiles

stamps and stickers

Styrofoam pieces

yarn

- Nature collages: Take children on a nature walk to collect natural materials to glue or paste onto card stock or cardboard. Help them flatten delicate items such as leaves and flowers by laying a sheet of newspaper and a heavy object over them. Alternatively, preserve them between two sheets of wax paper. Lay a piece of newspaper under and on top of the wax paper and iron the stack to melt the wax. Note: The iron is for adult use only.

- Paper-shapes collages: Provide an assortment of precut geometric shapes of different sizes and colors. Children can arrange the shapes to create designs before gluing

them in place. Keep markers and crayons handy for those who want to draw on top of their designs.

• Tissue-paper collages: Provide or let children cut or tear tissue paper of different colors into pieces. Give them sheets of heavy-weight paper, a bowl of liquid starch, paintbrushes, and glue sticks. Children can arrange the tissue on their papers, securing each piece with a glue stick. Alternatively, they can apply a thin layer of starch on their papers first, which will help keep the tissue paper in place. Once they are satisfied with their arrangements, they can apply another thin coat of liquid starch on top. Overlapping pieces of tissue produces combinations of colors. If wax paper is used as the base, the effect is rather like stained glass.

- Torn-paper collages: Children can tear assorted types of paper before pasting or gluing them onto their papers. When markers, crayons, or other collage materials are provided, they have the option of adding to their collages.

- Family-photo collages: Make copies of photographs of children and their families for them to cut out and arrange on paper to create individual photo "album" collages. Take dictation or help children label their collages identifying people, places, and events.

- Sandpaper and yarn collages: Provide sheets of coarse sandpaper and lengths of colored yarn. Children can arrange the yarn on the sandpaper which will "grab" it. The yarn can be taken off and rearranged as children play with their arrangements.

- Thematic collages: Supply pictures from magazines and calendars for children to cut out. The pictures can share a theme—for example, nature, faces, or animals—or children can select similar pictures from an assortment to create their own themes before arranging and gluing them into place.

- Jumbles: Provide containers of different kinds of materials for children to select and arrange in their own way. While too many materials can be confusing, including three to five kinds of materials that ordinarily would not be grouped together can lead to unexpected and innovative creations. For example, give children shells, pipe cleaners, paper clips, and cotton balls. Cardboard or card stock work well as the base, but pieces of fabric can also be used.

- Colored-squares mosaics: Cut one-inch squares from five or six different colors of construction paper. Provide glue and cotton swabs or glue sticks for children to use to secure their arrangements onto the background. Alternatively, cut magazine photos into squares.

- Graph-paper mosaics: Give children large-grid graph paper and colored markers. They can make mosaic patterns by coloring in the graph-paper squares.

- Plastic-lid mosaics: Provide shallow plastic lids, white glue, and bowls of seeds and other small items. Children can squeeze enough glue into each lid to completely cover the bottom before pressing the seeds or other items in place. Once their mosaics are dry, they can paint them with tempera paint. Paint added to the glue will make more colorful backgrounds. Alternatively, purchase tile adhesive from a hardware or dollar store to fill the lids. Provide sequins, beads, broken tiles, and glass nuggets.

Assemblages and Sculptures

Similar to collages, assemblages are pieces of artwork made from assorted items; but, like sculptures, they are more three-dimensional. Some assemblages and sculptures are created on a base such as florists' clay or Styrofoam. Others can be mounted on a base afterward. Items such as cardboard pieces, feathers, metal scraps, paper clips, pipe cleaners, and wire are easy to stick into the bases and rearranged during the creative process. Many materials can be used in assemblages and sculptures. Be on the lookout for one-of-a-kind and found items to add to your supplies. Enlist families' support in saving recycled materials such as the following.

berry baskets	milk cartons
bottle caps	paper cups
boxes	paper-towel rolls
bubble wrap	plastic cups, bottles, and lids
buttons	sewing notions
cardboard	thread spools
corks	toy blocks
egg-carton cups	wire
fabric scraps	wood scraps
florists' clay	wooden beads
metal scraps without sharp edges	

- Box art: Provide an assortment of boxes of different sizes and shapes, cardboard tubes, and cardboard egg-carton cups. After children tape and/or glue their materials together, provide paint and collage materials for adding details. Box art can inspire children to make houses or other types of structures.

- Hanger faces: Bend wire hangers into circles, keeping the hook at the top for hanging. Stretch and tie off pieces of pantyhose around the circles. Set out containers of buttons, fabric scraps, yarn, and glue for children to use to make faces on their hanger circles.

- Everything-but-the-kitchen-sink assemblages: As the name implies, materials that are suitable for this project include just about everything. Possibilities include different types of food containers and packaging parts, such as bottle caps, bread crimps, bubble wrap, and onion bags; small hardware and plumbing fittings; and broken toy pieces as well as the kinds of odds and ends that often end up in a kitchen junk drawer. Give children sturdy bases on which to create their assemblages along with glue, paste, or tape to stick materials they select together.

- Newspaper hats: For each child, use four sheets of newspaper. Lay them flat on a table with mismatched corners.

Place all four layers on each child's head. Use masking tape to circle the child's head like a crown. Remove the hat, roll up the edges, and tape them in place with small pieces of masking tape. Let the children paint their hats and/or decorate them with collage materials.

- Paper-bag sculptures: Help children stuff paper bags with crumpled up newspaper and tie the tops shut. These make good foundations for sculptures, and their shapes inspire innovation. Offer paint, glue or paste, and collage items for children to use to create their own sculptures.

- Wind chimes: Provide items that will make a sound when bumped together. Options include keys, wooden beads strung together, washers, old utensils, and CDs or DVDs, as well as shells, cans, or can lids with small holes drilled through them. Children can use acrylic paint or other materials to decorate some of these items first. Help them string or tie their selections onto varying lengths of cord and then tie each cord onto sturdy sticks or bundle the cords together and pull them through the holes of inverted flowerpots.

- Wire sculptures: Use wires that children can easily bend, such as pipe cleaners, garden wire, telephone cable wire (the colored wires inside the cables), or any 18- to 20-gauge wire cut into lengths that children are able to manage. Give them bases of Styrofoam or florists' clay into which they can push their wires. They can string buttons and beads on the wires or add fabric scraps, yarn, and feathers to complete their sculptures. Alternatively, nail or staple children's finished sculptures onto wood blocks after they have finished.

- Wood sculptures: Set out a variety of wooden beads, clothespins, spools, toy blocks, or wood scraps for this project. School-supply stores often sell boxes of small wooden pieces. Children can glue wooden items together on squares of heavy cardboard, Masonite, or matte board. If glue is insufficient for heavier pieces, use a glue gun to help them create their sculptures.

Outdoor Art Explorations

There are many ways for children to create art outside. Weather allowing, it is easy to take easels outside or simply set up art supplies on a picnic table. The outdoors can inspire children to express themselves in new ways. It is also a particularly good place for messy art projects.

- Sidewalk-chalk drawings: Sidewalk chalk is readily available at school-supply and craft stores. Besides drawing with dry chalk, children can dip chalk into water first to make the colors more vivid. Give children spray bottles filled with water. Once their sidewalk drawings are finished, they can spray them with water to blend the colors. Take children outdoors after a rainfall to draw on a wet sidewalk.

- Sidewalk paintings: Use the recipe for sidewalk paint in Appendix B. Give children paintbrushes, foam brushes, or sponges to paint the sidewalk with this mixture.

Alternatively, once their sidewalk paintings are finished, give children spray bottles filled with white vinegar. Spraying their paintings will make the colors fizz.

• Rock and flowerpot painting: Well-cleaned rocks or inverted flowerpots make unusual canvases. Let children paint on them with acrylic outdoor craft paint. If you also provide painters' tape, children can first apply strips to these forms before painting over them. Once their paintings have dried, remove any tape, and seal each with a coat of varnish.

• Packing-tape nature collages: Tape clear packaging tape to each child's wrist with the sticky side out. Take them on a nature walk. When they find natural materials they like, they can pick them up with their tape bracelets. Back inside, cut their bracelets so they can stick them onto paper.

- Mural painting: Pin or tape a length of easel or butcher paper to a fence. Set out small buckets of tempera paint for children to use to make a group mural. Any drips can be hosed down afterward.

- Spray painting: Hang a white sheet on a fence or pin it to a clothesline. Add about 2 tablespoons of liquid watercolor paint to one cup of water. Primary colors are best. Fill spray bottles with this solution. Let children squirt the sheet to blend colors and create interesting effects. Alternatively, give children strips of masking tape to tape on the sheet ahead of time. You can also use the tape to make square or rectangle frames for the paintings ahead of time. When the tape is removed, children's watercolor paintings will be highlighted. Lay a sheet or large piece of white paper on the ground, and provide assorted paper shapes and/or leaves. Children can arrange these on top of their canvasses before spraying over them with the watercolor solution.

- Paint with water: Simply give children buckets of water and large paintbrushes to "paint" the sidewalk and play-ground equipment.

Technology-Based Artwork

When chosen and employed with care, digital technology can expand children's creative arts experiences and means for self-expression. It can give children new ways to create art. However, any technology you select should be completely open ended so that it encourages children's experimentation, problem solving, and creativity.

- Computer software and apps: Graphic paint programs and drawing apps enable children to experiment with color, shapes, and lines to create original designs and pictures. To be truly open ended, these programs should allow children to start their creations from scratch so they can determine what and how they will draw or paint. There should also be options for using several drawing and painting tools. Many programs and apps on the market claim to be open ended, but only a few actually are. Many of the others feature cartoon-like characters that children can add to or manipulate. While choices are offered, these predrawn characters are products of the designers' imaginations, not the children's. Blank slate programs such as Kid Pix Deluxe, Paper by FiftyThree, or SketchBook Express are preferred. Software and apps like these enable children to create original artwork arising from their own ideas and feelings.

- Digital cameras: Stand-alone digital cameras or phones and tablets with built-in cameras are handy tools for photographing both children's work in progress as well as temporary works of art. For example, children's arrangements of natural items or colorful stones, block constructions, or nonhardened clay sculptures can be photographed and printed so the children can use the images in other art pieces. Most young children are capable of using the cameras themselves.

• Overhead projectors and document cameras: Overhead projectors shine images on transparencies or colors from color paddles or cellophane onto walls or screens to inspire children's artwork. Opaque objects placed on the glass create magnified shapes on the wall. More versatile document cameras allow both the magnification and projection of opaque images, colors, and shapes. These devices make it possible to show children a variety of prints of great artists' work. They also allow you to project children's own creations. A projector or document camera set up in the art center enables children to draw, experiment with colors, or create temporary collages without glue while observing the effects they can produce on a wall or screen.

• Interactive whiteboards: Touch-sensitive interactive whiteboards (IWBs) are less common and more complex than any of digital devices or projectors described above. An IWB is connected to a computer that in turn is connected to a projector, enabling the computer screen to be displayed on a four-to-six-foot white steel board. An IWB allows children to use their fingers or a special pen on the board instead of a computer keyboard or mouse. Many brands of IWBs come loaded with software, some of which are used for drawing-based activities with digital pens, pencils, highlighters, and erasers. Other separately purchased programs such as Kid Pix can also be used. The size of the board offers new possibilities for artistic expression. Children delight in using large, sweeping strokes to create images on the board, erasing and/or refining them as they draw. IWBs also encourage children to work together, increasing the likelihood they will talk with each other about their drawings. IWBs also allow children to insert written text, photos, videos, and recorded sounds and words into their work. Work can be saved to a file, printed, used for assessment, or to help children reflect on what they have created.

CHAPTER

6

Ideas for Music and Movement Experiences

Children use music and creative movement to interpret their experiences and communicate their feelings and ideas. They are instinctively drawn to all kinds of sounds and music. Perhaps with the exception of lullabies, most children cannot remain still when they hear music, particularly if it has a rhythmic tempo. While it is important to integrate music and movement instruction across the early childhood curriculum, it is equally important for children to experiment freely with the intertwined "languages" of music and movement. Listening to and making music and spontaneously using their bodies to respond to it stimulate brain connections. In the process, children develop and strengthen perceptual, cognitive, psychomotor, social, and emotional skills. Music and movement deepen their critical thinking and problem-solving skills and expand their aesthetic and cultural understandings. Most children will engage in music and movement experiences with joy and enthusiasm when the atmosphere is relaxed and they have time to express themselves in their own ways and at their own paces.

Think of creative movement as dance. It may not be dance of a conventional kind, but it is nonetheless an art form through which children respond expressively with their bodies. And because it capitalizes on children's natural inclinations to explore their environments with their bodies, it is inherently motivating. It helps children listen to and enjoy music even more. It provides a joyful release of energy while simultaneously allowing children to discover their physical and creative potentials and to refine fundamental movement skills, balance, and coordination. Every child, even those with physical challenges, can enjoy musical experiences and participate in expressing their feelings and ideas through movement. When there is no pressure to perform or to reach a set standard, children will feel successful and self-confident.

STIMULATING CREATIVE EXPRESSION THROUGH MUSIC AND MOVEMENT

Creating an environment and providing materials that inspire children to discover, analyze, and create are the first steps in helping them express themselves through these languages. In addition to arranging and equipping a music center where children explore and experiment with sound-making instruments, planned experiences and your guidance further encourage learning and creative expression. The most important considerations should be ensuring that music and movement experiences are playful, interactive, and joyful.

- **Play high-quality music.** Children frequently hear music. Popular culture is saturated with Top 40 songs, screen media soundtracks, advertisement jingles, and music played in shopping malls. But music of these kinds may lack quality and may not encourage children

to really listen. They may not have had opportunities to hear classical, jazz, or folk music, let alone music from a variety of cultures. Each piece of music is unique. Its rhythm, tempo, and mood suggest individual interpretation and expression through movement. It is up to you to expand children's musical diets and help them focus on, appreciate, and respond to what they hear in their own ways.

Good sources for high-quality music selections:

• Parents' Choice (http://www.parents-choice.org) lists award-winning audio selections.

• The National Association for the Education of Young Children website (http://families.naeyc.org/)

includes monthly collections of children's songs as well as an archive of past selections.

- Both Gryphon House (http://www.gryphonhouse.com) and Redleaf Press (http://www.redleafpress.org) sell CDs with excellent compilations of music and dance selections.

- Best Children's Music (http:// www. bestchildrensmusic.com) offers recommended high-quality music for children of different ages.

- Your local public library likely loans CDs of children's and other genres of music. The children's librarian can help you select ones that are appropriate for your class.

- **Encourage active listening.** Children are bombarded with sounds from all quarters. No wonder they sometimes tune out. To help them listen to, rather than just hear, particular pieces of music, ask, "How does it make you feel?" and "What does it remind you of?" Many young children find it easier to express their thoughts and feelings physically rather than verbally.

To help children focus attention and increase their abilities to distinguish and label particular sounds, guide them in sound explorations. Play matching games by shaking pairs of plastic film canisters filled with different items. Both indoors and outdoors, talk with them about what they hear when they close their eyes. Help them compare the loudness, pitch, and rhythm patterns of sounds. Ask them how many sounds they can make using only their hands or their mouths without their voices.

As they listen to music with a definite rhythm, ask them to clap or tap the beat. Talk with them about the various instruments they hear in pieces of music. Begin with simple instrumental pieces, those with only a few instruments. Then introduce more complex pieces. *Peter and the Wolf* by Sergey Prokofiev or *The Nutcracker* by Pyotr Tchaikovsky highlight particular instruments, making them easier to distinguish. If possible, demonstrate an instrument such as a guitar, tambourine, or bongo drum that is used in a piece of recorded music. Let children experiment with the different sounds they can make with it.

- **Establish basic ground rules for self-management.** Help children recognize auditory and visual cues for music and movement. Signals such as stopping the music, dimming lights, or shaking a tambourine help them know when to stop moving or making music.

To help them better understand personal-space boundaries and avoid conflicts, have each of them stand on a spot (a carpet square, a rubber dot, or a tape mark on the floor). Ask them to imagine they are bubbles. Have them touch all over the insides of their bubbles. With music playing, encourage them to dance inside their own bubbles to practice staying in their own spaces. Tell them that if their bubbles touch other bubbles, the bubbles will pop. Alternatively, use large plastic hoops to define individual space if children have trouble staying out of each other's way.

- **Balance individual, partner, and group activities.** As in other areas of the curriculum, it is most appropriate to balance teacher-directed activities (teaching a song), teacher-guided activities (playing a musical selection for children to interpret through movement), and child-initiated activities (free exploration in the music center). Whole-group music and movement experiences are common in early childhood curriculum. Although children benefit from adult guidance and enjoy these group experiences, creative expression stems from their own judgments about what to do and how to do it in the absence of teacher directions. They need time to explore, play with, and use sound-making materials in their own ways and at their own paces. They also need time to test and practice different ways to respond to music they choose.

- **Introduce new materials and activities.** To spark interest and encourage participation, introduce musical instruments one at a time before placing them in the music center. Demonstrate how to play each instrument and vary its sound. Ask children to compare what they hear when you pluck different strings on a guitar, strike the shortest and longest keys on the xylophone, blow forcefully and gently into a recorder, or tap a drum with your whole hand and then with just one finger. Place an easily operated CD or tape player in the music center for children to use to record and then listen to the music they make.

• **Provide props.** In addition to supplying instruments in the music center, include one or two broken or homemade microphones without a cord to stimulate children's songs and dance. (Save working electronic microphones for special occasions.) Simple props also support children's creative movement. They encourage exploration and inspire innovation, and they help self-conscious children feel more comfortable expressing themselves. Scarves, hoops, balls, jingle-bell wristbands, stuffed animals, and dolls make wonderful movement materials. Have children practice ways to use props for movement before making them available for independent use. For example, make a game out of dancing with scarves:

  • Hold your scarf with one hand and make it wiggle.

  • Hold it with two hands and make it flap like a flag on a flagpole.

  • Make it fly like a kite.

  • Make it float like a snowflake.

  • Toss it in the air and catch it.

  • Hold opposite ends with a partner and dance together.

Natural items and repurposed household materials are easily turned into instruments and dance props for children to use. For example, children can create "dance partners" by gluing fabric skirts and hats onto empty detergent bottles.

- **Join in.** Let go of your inhibitions. Your active involvement in music and movement helps children feel free to express themselves. Sing and dance enthusiastically with children. Close your classroom door if that makes you more comfortable. Regardless of how you sound or look, children will catch your spirit and be eager to participate. When you encourage children to interpret music through movement, do the same. If the whole class is lying on the floor drawing what music sounds like to them, join in by drawing alongside them.

- **Use open-ended questions and comments.** To deepen critical thinking and problem solving, use open-ended questions and comments to help children focus on musical elements such as dynamics, tempo, pitch, and rhythm.

  - *I hear you shaking the maraca in time to the music.*

  - *Show how you can make the beat faster.*

  - *I see you're tiptoeing when the music is soft.*

  - *What do you hear in the music that makes you move so quickly?*

  - *What would happen if you tapped your drum with your fingers? How does it sound different from when you use the stick? Can you find other things to beat it with to change the sound?*

- **Recognize music and movement expression.** Provide responsive feedback when children sing, play instruments, and dance. Record their explorations, and play back the recordings to help children revisit and extend what they have done. Share the recordings with families.

- **Invite family and community members to share music or dance talents.** Music is a significant part of every culture's heritage. Draw on local resources to broaden children's appreciation and prompt their creativity. Ask parents and other family members to sing traditional songs, play instruments, or dance for the children. If they are not able to do so in person, ask to borrow any recordings of music they have. Integrate music from a variety of cultures to promote cultural identity and encourage appreciation of others.

  Give older siblings who are learning to play instruments opportunities to give informal recitals for your class. Take children to watch the high school marching band practice.

- **Observe and document children's responses.** Pay attention to those aspects of music and movement experiences to which children are particularly responsive. Document individual reactions to musical genres, props and instruments, and styles of expression. Incorporate these in future activities to further motivate and extend creative expression and increase self-confidence.

- **Include music and creative movement throughout the day.** Music and movement help make classrooms joyful places. They enhance topical investigations and thematic studies. They ease transitions and make these kinds of activities more fun. Incorporate them in classroom routines. For example, accompany cleanup and hand washing with song. Help children walk in line by pretending to be train cars or one long caterpillar. Ask them to shake like bowls of jelly or repeat a rhythm you clap while waiting to be picked up.

ACTIVITIES AND MATERIALS

Whole-Group Activities

- Music Moves Me: Play music with different tempos, rhythms, and moods. There are many possibilities: jazz, lullabies, marches, polkas, waltzes, reggae, Hawaiian, Latin, African, Native American, or Asian cultural selections. Encourage children to listen to and move in the way the music makes them feel. If this is a new kind of experience, ask just two or three dancers to begin. Others can gradually join in, or children can take turns dancing while other children watch.

- Imagination Movers: Ask children to move like the wind, a cloud, an airplane, popping corn, jiggling gelatin, a galloping horse, a hopping frog, a slithering snake, or their favorite animal. Ask them to creep, twirl, bounce, stomp, move in slow motion, or as if they have stepped on hot asphalt.

- Musical Animals: Play classical music pieces that evoke particular animals for children to interpret through movement. Selections with animal themes include:

  - "Flight of the Bumblebee" by Nikolai Rimsky-Korsakov

  - *Babar the Elephant* by Francis Poulenc

  - *The Gadfly Suite* by Dmitri Shostakovich

  - *The Carnival of the Animals* by Camille Saint-Saëns

  - *The Thieving Magpie* by Gioachino Rossini

  - *The Red Pony* by Aaron Copland

  - *The Birds* by Ottorino Respighi

  - *The Firebird* by Igor Stravinsky

- I'm Stuck! To encourage problem solving and discovery of movement possibilities, have children "glue" different body parts to the floor while they move. Start with just their feet, then just their knees and lower legs, and then move on to hands, elbows, and bottoms.

- Color Dances: Project different colors onto a screen using color paddles or colored cellophane. Encourage children to move the way each color makes them feel.

- Shadow Dancing: Shine a spotlight or an overhead projector lamp onto a screen or plain wall. Turn off the other lights, and turn on the music. When children move between the light and the screen, they will see their shadows dance. Hang a sheet from the ceiling with enough space behind it for half the children to sit. Shine the light onto the sheet. Divide children into groups with dancers on the lighted side and the audience on the other. As you play different pieces of music, the dancers' shadows will be projected onto the sheet for the audience to see. Give each group a turn. Simple props such as scarves or hats will extend this experience. Ask some of the children to be musicians accompanying you on their instruments as you alter the beat of a drum for the dancers.

- Flashlight Dancing: Darken the room. Slowly move the beam of a flashlight across the floor. Children can move into or across the beam to dance as the music plays.

- Story Dances: Retell a familiar story or recite a favorite poem that has descriptive imagery. As you play music softly in the background, encourage the children to interpret the story or poem through movement. Alternatively, play or sing songs that include actions to inspire their creative movement.

- Skating to Music: Give each child two paper plates, one for each foot. With these paper plate "skates" under their feet, they can slide and glide to music. Make sure there is adequate space without obstacles in the way.

Music and Movement Activities

- Statues: Whenever the music pauses, children stop dancing. Tell them they must "freeze" like statues and hold their poses until the music starts.

- Popping Bubbles: Give each child a sheet of bubble wrap with large bubbles to place on the floor. Explain that when the music plays, they can pop the bubbles using as many parts of their bodies as they can except for their hands. They must stop popping when the music stops.

- Animal Dreams: Have children lay their heads on the floor while you sing, "Sleeping, sleeping, all the children are sleeping. They are dreaming about being . . . cats." On the word *cats*, they get up and move like cats. Start over and change the name of the animal to bees, kangaroos, caterpillars, and so on. End the game with children once again pretending to sleep.

- Instrument Guessing Game: After children have explored a variety of instruments in the music center, place several different instruments on opposite sides of a table divided by a tri-fold board. Have two children sit on different sides of the table so they cannot see each other. They can take turns playing an instrument for the other child to identify.

- Mirrors: Show children how their reflections in a mirror make the same movements as they do. Then ask them to pretend they are mirrors reflecting the movements you make. Pair children so they can take turns being mirrors trying to reproduce each other's movements. Start with facial expressions, then hands and arms, and finally with feet and legs.

- Two Make a Shape: Ask pairs of children to make a shape together that a particular piece of music makes them think of. They may decide to form geometric, animal, or letter shapes. When you change the music, challenge them to change their shapes.

- Sunny-Day Shadows: Encourage children to watch their shadows as they dance together in the sunlight. Ask in how many ways they can make their shadows touch each other's shadow.

Individual and Small-Group Activities

- Music Laboratory: Stock your music center with basic instruments so children can experiment with sounds and invent their own music. Teach them how to use a CD or cassette player to record their music. Post illustrated instructions.

- All Kinds of Bells: Place an assortment of bells in the music center—jingle bells, hand bells, cowbells, resonator tubes, and bells of different sizes and materials. Encourage children to compare their sounds. Ask them to categorize them in different ways and to sequence them by pitch.

- Musical Art: Play different musical selections for children. Encourage them to draw or paint what they hear. When appropriate, take dictation or help them label their creations.

- Kitchen Gadget Band: Lay an assortment of common kitchen utensils and equipment on a blanket in the music center. Items such as pans, plastic bowls, wooden spoons, an eggbeater, flour sifter, spatula, cheese grater, pot scrubber, and wire strainer work well. Let children experiment with the sounds they can make with these items.

- Musical Theater: Turn the music center into a musical theater complete with a stage area, costume clothing, instruments with which children are familiar, and microphones. Add carpet squares or chairs for the audience and tickets for the ticket sellers.

- Favorite-Song Pictures: Have children choose a favorite song to illustrate. They may choose to work on their illustrations alone, or several children can create a group mural of the song or illustrate separate verses of it.

- Scarf Dancing: Place colorful, lightweight scarves in a basket or tub in an area with a full-length nonbreakable mirror. Play different kinds of instrumental music to inspire dancing.

- Tabletop Rhythm: Completely cover a table with sheets of newspaper or easel paper. Give each child a marker or crayon. Play music on a CD or tape. Let the children walk around the table moving their markers on the paper to the beat of the music. Vary the types of music you play and/or stop the music altogether so that children "freeze" before you start it up again.

- Playground Orchestra: Take a basket of instruments outside. Set them up on a blanket or place them in a playhouse. The playground is the perfect place for children to beat drums of all kinds and to otherwise express themselves exuberantly through music! Hang sound makers from trees or playground equipment, making sure they pose no safety hazards. Old pots and lids, broiler pans, hubcaps, metal spoons, water bottles filled with pebbles, driftwood, and plastic buckets work well for this sound garden. Suspend graduated lengths of PVC pipe or bamboo to make a vertical xylophone. Permanently mount metal items to posts or wooden fences. After children have had ample time to experiment with making sounds, record their musical creations.

Projects

Recycled and repurposed household items are easily combined to make simple props and instruments.

- Dancing Streamers: Punch several holes on the edges of paper plates or similarly sized pieces of cardboard. After children have decorated their plates, help them attach crepe-paper streamers through the holes. Turn the music on or take the children onto the playground (or both!) so they can dance with their streamers.

- Shakers: Let children put a little birdseed or some pebbles in plastic water or salad-dressing bottles. Supply beads or confetti to make their shakers more colorful. Seal the tops with masking or duct tape. Encourage them to compare the different sounds their shakers make, particularly if several kinds of materials are available.

- Shoe-box Guitars: Cut a large hole in the center of each box lid. After the children have decorated their boxes with crayons, markers, or paint, tape the lids on tightly. Help them wrap four to six strong rubber bands lengthwise around their boxes. In general, the thicker the rubber band, the louder and the lower the sound will be when it is plucked. For clearer sounds, place a pencil just under the rubber bands on one side of the lid. When the pencil is moved, the rubber-band strings will provide different notes. Other small sturdy boxes can also be used.

- Spin Drums: Give children heavy paper plates to decorate on both sides with crayons, markers, or paint. Poke a hole in the rim on opposite sides of each plate. Cut lengths of string about 2 inches longer than the distance from the rim to the center of the plates. Help children tie a string through each hole. Then help them tie a bead onto the end of each string. Cut two slits about 1 inch in length into opposite sides of paper-towel rolls. Help children squeeze glue into the slits and then push their paper plates into the slits so they are centered halfway between the beaded strings. Use a glue gun if necessary. The finished spin drums should resemble lollipops. When children turn the handles back and forth, the beads will hit the centers of their drums creating rhythmic beats that inspire movement.

- Paper-Plate Maracas: Fold paper plates in half. Help children fill their plates about halfway with dried beans or rice. Staple the plates shut and tape over the staples. Provide crayons, markers, and/or paint for children to use to decorate their maracas, along with ribbon or crepe-paper streamers. Help children staple ribbons or crepe-paper streamers to the edges. Two paper plates stapled together will make circular maracas.

- Papier-Mâché Maracas: Show children how to cover already-inflated balloons with several layers of papier-mâché, leaving the tied ends uncovered. Once these forms are completely dry, snip the ends off and help children pour birdseed into the cavities. Securely tape pencils or tongue depressors into the holes. Provide tempera paint for children to decorate their maracas. Once they are dry, spray them with hairspray to seal the paint. *Caution: Keep uninflated balloons and pieces away from children, as they can be a choking hazard.*

• Oatmeal-Box Drums: Cut both ends off oatmeal containers. Encourage children to decorate their boxes however they wish. For each drum, cut the neck of a balloon off, and help children stretch the remaining part over each end of their containers, securing them with rubber bands. Provide pencils for children to beat on their drums in time to music.

• Rainmakers: Give children cardboard tubes to personalize in their own way. Help them securely tape a circle of construction paper or card stock cut the same size as the tube's opening onto one end. Provide cups of rice or dry beans for children to pour into their tubes; a funnel will make this easier. The more rice or beans they add, the louder the sounds their rainmakers will make. Help them tape a second circle of paper or card stock to the other end. When they hold their rainmakers vertically and then turn them over, the falling rice or beans will sound like rain.

• Stamping Sticks: Percussion instruments known as stamping sticks are used by a variety of cultures around the world. They are pounded on the ground to make rhythms. Children can create stamping sticks by using tape to cover only one end of a paper-towel, wrapping-paper, or carpet tube. Let children personalize their stamping sticks before banging them on different surfaces to vary the sounds they can make. Sounds will be magnified by traveling up the insides of their tubes.

- Paper-Towel Roll Kazoos: For each kazoo, cut a circle of wax paper about 1 inch in circumference larger than the end of the paper roll. With the child's help, place the wax paper over the end of the roll, and wrap a rubber band around it to secure it tightly. Punch a hole with a pair of scissors in one side of the paper roll about one-and-a-half inches from the wax-paper end. Children can decorate their kazoos with markers and stickers before humming or singing into them with the wax-paper side pressed up against their lips.

- Jam-Jar Xylophone: Fill six to eight glass jars, cups, or bottles of similar sizes with different amounts of water. Add food coloring to the water if you wish. Line up the jars from the least to the most amount of water. Encourage children to experiment with sounds by using spoons, chopsticks, or wooden mallets to tap the glasses. Ask them to compare the sound each jar makes. Challenge them to create their own tunes.

- Tin-Can Xylophone: Collect and clean eight to twelve tin cans that are of the same height but of several different diameters. Be sure there are no rough edges. Rubber band or tape two cans together. Add more cans, securing them with rubber bands or tape. If you have a big can, it works well as the center of a circle of cans. Let children experiment with sounds by hitting the inverted cans with the eraser ends of pencils.

• Socket-Wrench Xylophone: Invert a cardboard egg carton. Lay graduated socket wrenches widthwise in the spaces between the egg cups. Children can use spoons or wooden mallets to play the xylophone. Suggest that they rearrange the wrenches to further compare their tones.

• Metal Wind Chime: Provide an assortment of small metal items such as washers, keys, old jewelry, or ring fasteners. Help the children thread ribbons of about equal lengths through the holes and then tie their items onto metal hangers, sticks, or dowels that they have painted or wrapped with colored tape. Clean tin cans with holes drilled in the bottom also work well. Ribbons tied to both ends of the sticks or dowels and then to each other allow the chimes to be hung.

• Bead Chime: For each wind chime, punch four holes around the rim of a paper cup. Give children tempera or acrylic paint to make designs on their cups. Provide an assortment of beads with large holes, drinking straws cut into pieces, and string cut to desired lengths. Children can alternately thread the beads and straw onto four pieces of string, leaving about 2 inches at the top of each string so it can be tied into one of the holes in the cup. Help each child make a small loop in one end of a pipe cleaner. Tie a string about 2 inches longer than the others through this loop. Poke a hole in the center of the cup's base and push the straight end of the pipe cleaner through the hole so that the loop acts as a stopper. Tie a metal washer on the end of this middle string so that it is about the same length as the beaded strings. Make another loop in the top of the pipe cleaner to make a handle. When the wind blows, the washer will hit the beaded strings, making them chime.

- Musical Instrument Factory: Encourage children to make their own instruments using assorted recycled items such as aluminum pans, tin cans, bottle caps, crinkly cellophane, buttons, short lengths of PVC pipe, cardboard rolls, spoons, chopsticks, sandpaper, or plastic containers. After they have explored the possibilities, help them tape items together. Alternatively, provide only natural items such as pinecones, seedpods, acorns, and sticks along with several kinds of containers. Give children opportunities to share and talk about their instruments with the group.

Technology in Music and Movement

When making decisions about when and how to use technology in music and movement experiences, ask yourself to what extent it will encourage each child's creative expression.

To bring a variety of music into the classroom, audio equipment is essential. Teachers can operate CD or tape players or digital devices such as iPods and other MP3 players with connected speakers during whole-group activities. But music centers equipped with audio devices that children can manage themselves create exciting opportunities for music and movement experiences. Individual audio and other technological devices extend children's musical repertoires and provide them a means to generate their own forms of music and dance. Songs and music played on CD, tape, and MP3 players, and even on karaoke machines, motivate engagement. Headphones give children individual choices, reduce distractions, and extend listening times. They also make it possible for an individual child to draw or paint his ideas about a piece of music while he listens. Headphones connected to a simple electronic keyboard enable children to explore and experiment with sounds and make music without disturbing others.

Internet searches help you show children music and dance performances beyond the classroom or their communities or cultures. Sampling from an online site also enables you to preview and download songs and appropriate pieces of music without purchasing an entire CD. Standalone digital cameras or phones and tablets with built-in cameras make it easy for both you and the children to capture creative expression through music and movement. The resulting images and video footage enable children to review and extend what they have done. They can also be shared with families and combined to make video montages.

CHAPTER
7

Family Connections and Spreading the Word

Once you have observed how powerful creative play is as a medium for children's learning, I hope you feel compelled to spread the word to families, colleagues, and supervisors. You are an advocate for dramatic play, art, music, and movement expression when you share with others concrete evidence of how children benefit. Many adults, parents included, continue to think of learning as separate from creative, self-regulated activities. It is up to you to help them understand the direct links between the two. The best ways to do this are to show rather than tell and to enable them to experience first-hand children's engagement in learning through play.

Sharing Children's Play and Creations

Concrete evidence in the forms of captioned photographs, narrated videos, and children's explanations of their work help others understand that creative play is about thinking and communicating ideas. There are many ways to share this evidence with others.

Post photos in entryways and other areas where parents are most likely to see them. Include photos of children engaged in dramatic play, creating art, making music, or dancing together. Attach descriptions to help others connect the images with the development of concepts, skills, and dispositions. Consider displaying a series of photos showing the sequences of children's sustained play or the steps they used to make something original. Add brief narratives about what you observed. If possible, include children's explanations of the processes they used. After families have had a chance to look at the photos, place them in a binder in the same area. This binder will become a chronological photo journal of learning through creative play.

Photos and videos make great additions to online newsletters and classroom or school websites. In accounts of classroom events, include those that demonstrate engagement in dramatic play and other creative activities. Provide an explanation of what each image or video indicates and why it is important.

You may choose to highlight prosocial behavior, skill mastery, self-regulation, persistence, innovation, or simply children's delight in their own discoveries and accomplishments.

Best wishes in all your endeavors to promote joyful learning through play!

APPENDIX A: RECOMMENDED CHILDREN'S BOOKS

There are children's books related to every conceivable topic, theme, and issue of interest to young children. Many of them appeal to children's imaginations, sense of humor, and concerns. A few that are particularly helpful for inspiring children's creative expression are listed below.

Books to Inspire Dramatic Play

Ajmera, Maya, Elise Derstine, and Cynthia Pon. 2012. *What We Wear: Dressing Up Around the World.* Washington, DC: The Global Fund for Children.

Auerbach, Annie, and Rob Scotton. 2013. *Splat the Cat: On with the Show.* New York: HarperCollins.

Brown, Marcia. 1947. *Stone Soup.* New York: Simon and Schuster.

Cartlidge, Michelle. 1992. *Mouse Theater.* New York: Dutton Juvenile.

Charlip, Remy. 1964. *Fortunately.* New York: Simon and Schuster.

D'Amico, Carmela, and Steven D'Amico. 2006. *Ella Sets the Stage.* New York: Scholastic.

Davidson, Rebecca. 2003. *All the World's a Stage.* New York: HarperCollins.

Gibbons, Gail. 1996. *How a House Is Built.* New York: Holiday House.

Hoffman, Mary. 1991. *Amazing Grace.* New York: Dial Books for Young Readers.

Kane, Tracy. 2006. *Fairy Houses . . . Everywhere!* Lee, NH: Light-Beams.

Lodding, Linda. 2014. *A Gift for Mama*. New York: Alfred A. Knopf.

Nakagawa, Chihiro. 2008. *Who Made This Cake?* Honesdale, PA: Front Street.

Oxenbury, Helen, and Michael Rosen. 1997. *We're Going on a Bear Hunt*. New York: Margaret K. McElderry.

Perry, Sarah. 1995. *If . . .* Los Angeles, CA: Getty Trust.

Raffi. 1998. *Wheels on the Bus*. New York: Crown.

Slobodkina, Esphyr. 1987. *Caps for Sale: A Tale of a Peddler, Some Monkeys, and Their Monkey Business*. New York: HarperCollins.

Thomson, Sarah. 2005. *Imagine a Day*. New York: Atheneum Books for Young Readers.

Books Related to Art

Ahlberg, Allan. 2012. *The Pencil*. Cambridge, MA: Candlewick.

Aliki. 1988. *How a Book Is Made*. New York: HarperCollins.

Anholt, Laurence. 2007. *The Magical Garden of Claude Monet*. Hauppauge, NY: Barron's Educational.

Anholt, Laurence. 2007. *Matisse: The King of Color*. Hauppauge, NY: Barron's Educational.

Anholt, Laurence. 2007. *Picasso and the Girl with a Ponytail*. Hauppauge, NY: Barron's Educational.

Anholt, Laurence. 2007. *van Gogh and the Sunflowers*. Hauppauge, NY: Barron's Educational.

Aston, Diana Hutts. 2011. *Dream Something Big*. New York: Dial.

Banyai, Istvan. 1998. *Re-Zoom*. New York: Puffin.

Beaty, Andrea. 2007. *Iggy Peck, Architect*. New York: Harry N. Abrams.

Blizzard, Gladys. 1992. *Come Look with Me: Animals in Art*. Watertown, MA: Charlesbridge.

Carle, Eric. 2011. *The Artist Who Painted a Blue Horse* (*El artista que pintó un caballo azul*.) New York: Philomel.

Collins, Pat Lowery. 1994. *I Am an Artist*. Minneapolis, MN: Millbrook.

Daywalt, Drew. 2013. *The Day the Crayons Quit*. New York: Philomel.

dePaola, Tomie. 2001. *The Art Lesson*. New York: Paperstar.

Ehlert, Lois. 2014. *The Scraps Book: Notes from a Colorful Life*. New York: Beach Lane.

Gerstein, Mordicai. 2013. *The First Drawing*. New York: Little, Brown.

Hoban, Tana. 1998. *So Many Circles, So Many Squares*. New York: Greenwillow.

Hoban, Tana. 1996. *Shapes, Shapes, Shapes*. New York: Greenwillow.

Johnson, Crockett. 1960. *A Picture for Harold's Room*. New York: HarperCollins.

Johnson, Crockett. 1955. *Harold and the Purple Crayon*. New York: HarperCollins.

Leonni, Leo. 1991. *Matthew's Dream*. New York: Alfred A. Knopf.

Light, Kelly. 2014. *Louise Loves Art*. New York: Balzer and Bray.

Locker, Thomas, and Candace Christiansen. 2001. *Sky Tree*. New York: HarperCollins.

Mayhew, James. 2013. *Katie and the Starry Night*. London, UK: Hodder and Stoughton.

Mayhew, James. 2012. *Katie and the Waterlily Pond: A Magical Journey through Five Monet Masterpieces*. London, UK: Hodder and Stoughton.

Reynolds, Peter. 2012. *Sky Color*. Cambridge, MA: Candlewick.

Reynolds, Peter. 2004. *Ish*. Cambridge, MA: Candlewick.

Rosenstock, Barb. 2014. *The Noisy Paint Box: The Colors and Sounds of Kandinsky's Abstract Art*. New York: Knopf Books for Young Readers.

Russell, Natalie. 2014. *Lost for Words*. Atlanta, GA: Peachtree.

Saltzberg, Barney. 2012. *Andrew Drew and Drew*. New York: Harry N. Abrams.

Saltzberg, Barney. 2010. *Beautiful Oops!* New York: Workman.

Scanlon, Liz Garton. 2012. *Think Big*. New York: Bloomsbury USA.

Sohi, Morteza. 1995. *Look What I Did with a Leaf!* New York: Walker and Company.

Tullet, Hervé. 2014. *Mix It Up!* San Francisco, CA: Chronicle.

Warhola, James. 2005. *Uncle Andy's*. New York: Puffin.

Wiesner, David. 2010. *Art and Max*. New York: Clarion.

Wiesner, David. 1999. *Sector 7*. New York: Clarion.

Winter, Jeanette. 2013. *Henri's Scissors*. New York: Beach Lane.

Books Related to Music and Movement

Ackerman, Karen. 1992. *Song and Dance Man.* New York: Dragonfly.

Aliki. 2005. *Ah, Music!* New York: HarperCollins.

Andreae, Giles. 2012. *Giraffes Can't Dance.* New York: Cartwheel.

Boynton, Sandra. 2014. *The Bunny Rabbit Show!* New York: Workman.

Copeland, Misty. 2014. *Firebird.* New York: G. P. Putnam's Sons.

Cox, Judy. 2005. *My Family Plays Music.* New York: Holiday House.

Craig, Lindsey. 2012. *Dancing Feet!* New York: Knopf.

Curtis, Gavin. 2001. *The Bat Boy and His Violin.* New York: Aladdin.

Dillon, Leo, and Diane Dillon. 2002. *Rap a Tap Tap: Here's Bojangles—Think of That!* New York: Blue Sky.

Ehlert, Lois. 2005. *Leaf Man.* New York: Harcourt.

Ehrhardt, Karen. 2006. *The Jazz Man.* Orlando, FL: Harcourt.

Feiffer, Jules. 2014. *Rupert Can Dance.* New York: Farrar, Straus, and Giroux.

Gray, Libba Moore. 1999. *My Mama Had a Dancing Heart.* New York: Orchard.

Guidone, Thea. 2010. *Drum City.* Berkeley, CA: Tricycle.

Idle, Molly. 2013. *Flora and the Flamingo.* San Francisco, CA: Chronicle.

Isadora, Rachel. 1991. *Ben's Trumpet.* New York: Greenwillow.

Jonas, Ann. 1989. *Color Dance.* New York: Greenwillow.

Landalf, Helen, and Pamela Gerke. 1996. *Movement Stories for Children Ages 3–6*. Portland, ME: Smith and Kraus.

Lies, Brian. 2014. *Bats in the Band*. Boston, MA: Houghton Mifflin Harcourt.

Martin, Bill, Jr., and John Archambault. 1989. *Chicka Chicka Boom Boom*. New York: Simon and Schuster.

Martin, Bill, Jr., and John Archambault. 1988. *Barn Dance!* New York: Henry Holt.

Moss, Lloyd. 2000. *Zin! Zin! Zin! A Violin*. New York: Aladdin.

Prelutsky, Jack. 2010. *The Carnival of the Animals*. New York: Alfred A. Knopf.

Schaefer, Elizabeth. 2014. *Peppa Pig: Ballet Lesson*. New York: Scholastic.

Sif, Birgitta. 2014. *Frances Dean Who Loved to Dance and Dance*. Cambridge, MA: Candlewick.

Wheeler, Lisa. 2007. *Jazz Baby*. Orlando, FL: Harcourt.

Willems, Mo. 2012. *Listen to My Trumpet!* New York: Disney-Hyperion.

Willems, Mo. 2009. *Elephants Cannot Dance!* New York: Disney-Hyperion.

Wright, Johanna. 2014. *The Orchestra Pit*. New York: Roaring Brook.

APPENDIX B:
RECIPES FOR ART MATERIALS

Although recipes for homemade art materials are readily available on the Internet and from other sources, here are a few to consider.

Basic Fingerpaint

1/2 cup liquid tempera paint

1/2 liquid starch

Bowl

Mix liquid tempera paint with liquid starch.

Easy Clean-Up Fingerpaint

1/2 cup liquid tempera

2 Tbsp. liquid dish soap

Bowl

Mix liquid tempera paint with liquid soap.

Nontoxic Watercolor Paint

4 Tbsp. baking soda

2 Tbsp. white vinegar

2 Tbsp. cornstarch

1/2 tsp. light corn syrup

Ice cube tray or muffin tin

Liquid food coloring

Bowl

Combine baking soda and white vinegar. Add cornstarch and light corn syrup. Fill compartments of an ice cube tray or muffin tin just halfway. Add drops of food coloring to each compartment to obtain the desired colors. Let the paint dry completely in the containers so that it makes a cake. (This can take up to two days.) To use the paint, dip a paintbrush in a cup of clean water and rub it over a colored cake.

Bubble Solution

1/4 cup liquid dish soap

2 1/4 cups water

2 Tbsp. glycerin (available in drug stores)

Food coloring or dry tempera paint

Bowl

Mix liquid dishwashing detergent with water and glycerin. The solution can be colored with food coloring or dry tempera paint, which is better for making bubble prints.

Sidewalk Paint

1/2 cup water per color

1/2 cup cornstarch per color

Small lidded jars (one for each color)

Food coloring

Mix water with cornstarch in each jar. Then stir in 10-20 drops of food coloring.

Fizzy Sidewalk Paint

1 box baking soda

1/2 cup cornstarch

1/2 cup water

Food coloring

Spray bottle

White vinegar

Bowl

Put 10-20 drops of food coloring in water. Combine baking soda and cornstarch, and then add the diluted food coloring. If the consistency is too thick, add a little more water a spoonful at a time. Fill a spray bottle with white vinegar. After painting, the children can spray their sidewalk creations with the vinegar to make them fizz.

Foam Paint

White glue

White shaving cream

Food coloring

Bowl or ziplock bag

Sturdy paper or cardboard

Mix equal parts white glue and white shaving cream. Add food coloring. If a ziplock bag is used instead of a bowl to mix the ingredients, a corner of the bag can be snipped off so children can squeeze the paint onto sturdy paper or cardboard.

Snow Paint

White glue

White shaving cream

Bowl

Mix equal parts white glue with white shaving cream. It will dry soft and spongy.

Puffy Paint

1 cup flour

2 tsp. baking powder

1 tsp. salt

Water

Ziplock bags

Food coloring

Bowl

Mix flour, baking powder, salt, and enough water so the mixture is the consistency of pancake batter. Divide it into several ziplock bags, add food coloring, and squish the bags to distribute the color evenly. Snip a tiny hole in one corner of each bag so that paint can be squeezed through it.

Microwave Puffy Paint

1/4 cup self-rising flour

1/4 cup table salt

3/4 cup water

Food coloring

Card stock or cardboard

Microwave-safe dish

Add food coloring to the water. Combine self-rising flour, table salt, and the diluted food coloring. Paint it on card stock or cardboard. After each painting is finished, place it in a microwave-safe dish, and microwave it about 20–40 seconds. The paint will puff up. Avoid overcooking.

Uncooked Playdough

2 1/2 cups flour

1/2 cup salt

1 Tbsp. alum

2 cups boiling water (adult only)

3 Tbsp. vegetable oil or baby oil

Food coloring or 2 pkgs. flavored drink mix

Bowl

Mix flour, salt and alum. **Adult only:** Stir in boiling water, vegetable oil, and either food coloring or flavored drink mix. When cool enough to touch, knead until smooth. If you use baby oil, the dough will smell nice, not get rancid, and be less susceptible to mold. **Caution:** Inhaling baby oil can be fatal.

Cooked Playdough

1 cup white flour

1/2 cup salt

2 Tbsp. cream of tartar

1 cup water

1 Tbsp. oil

2 tsp. food coloring

Saucepan

Bowl

TIP:
When stored in the refrigerator in airtight containers such as ziplock bags, any of these modeling materials will keep for at least several days.

Mix flour, salt, and cream of tartar in a saucepan. In a separate bowl, combine water, oil, and food coloring. Add wet ingredients to dry ingredients. **Adult only:** Stir mixture over medium heat for 3–5 minutes until mixture forms a ball. Turn it out onto a lightly floured surface, and knead until smooth and no longer sticky.

Super-Soft Playdough

10–20 drops of food coloring

1 cup hair conditioner

2 cups cornstarch

Bowl

Add food coloring to hair conditioner. Slowly add cornstarch and mix until it comes together. Knead the mixture into a smooth ball. Add extra cornstarch if the mixture feels a little too sticky. Store in an airtight container or ziplock bag. This playdough works particularly well with cookie cutters.

Cloud Dough

4 cups of white flour

1/2 cup baby oil

Bowl

Mix flour with baby oil. Knead until smooth. **Caution:** Inhaling baby oil can be fatal.

Salt Dough

1 cup salt

2 cups flour

1 cup water

Bowl

Food coloring (optional)

Oil of cloves or oil of wintergreen (optional)

Mix salt, flour, water, and food coloring if desired. To help preserve the dough, add a few drops of oil of cloves or oil of wintergreen. Add slightly more of the salt, flour, or water if mixture is either too sticky or too dense. Knead until smooth.

Paintable Clay Dough

1 1/2 cups flour

1 cup salt

1 cup cornstarch

Warm water

Bowl

Mix flour, salt, and cornstarch. Slowly add warm water until the mixture holds a shape but is still easy to mold. Knead until smooth. Depending on the size of the creation, this clay will take 1–2 days to harden. Finished pieces can be painted.

Baking Soda Clay

2 cups baking soda

1 cup cornstarch

1 1/4 cup water

Food coloring

Saucepan

Mix baking soda, cornstarch, and water in a saucepan. Add food coloring. **Adult only:** Cook over medium heat, stirring constantly, until the mixture is the consistency of mashed potatoes. This will take 10–15 minutes. Once the mixture is cool enough to touch, knead it until smooth. Finished products can be dried overnight or in a very low-temperature oven.

Papier-Mâché Solution

White flour

Water

Bowl

Electric mixer (adult only)

Combine approximately 1 part flour with 2 parts water. Add the water slowly until the mixture is the consistency of white glue. Using an electric mixer will ensure a smooth paste.

APPENDIX C: ONLINE RESOURCES

A huge number of websites for educators and parents can be found on the Internet. Not all of them contain sound guidance or appropriate resources for supporting young children's creative expression. Among those that do are the following.

Alliance for Childhood

http://www.allianceforchildhood.org

Promotes policies and practices to support healthy development and restore active play in childhood.

American Association for the Child's Right to Play (IPA/USA)

http://www.ipausa.org

An international forum and advocacy organization promoting opportunities for play.

Arts Education Partnership (AEP)

http://www.aep-arts.org

Provides information and advocacy about making the arts an essential part of every child's education.

Association for Childhood Education International (ACEI)

http://www.acei.org

Disseminates and advocates for quality educational content for children around the world.

Campaign for a Commercial-Free Childhood (CCFC)

http://www.commercialfreechildhood.org

Works to reclaim childhood from corporate marketers.

Defending the Early Years (DEY)

http://deyproject.org

Advocates for appropriate practices in early childhood classrooms, especially play-based experiential learning, and supports educators in counteracting factors that undermine appropriate practice.

International Child Art Foundation (ICAF)

http://www.icaf.org

Devoted to supporting children's creative and empathetic development.

The J. Paul Getty Museum

http://www.getty.edu/museum

Offers information and resources for K–12 teachers and families to advance art education, along with art activities and lesson plans for students at different levels.

National Art Education Association (NAEA)

http://www.arteducators.org

Focus is visual arts education. It provides research articles about child development and the impact of visual arts. Members can access lesson and unit plans.

National Association for the Education of Young Children (NAEYC)

http://www.naeyc.org

The world's largest organization acting on behalf of young children. It publishes numerous top-quality resources for those teaching and caring for children from birth through age eight.

National Association for Music Education (NAfME)

http://www.nafme.org

Provides support and resources for educators and families for music education as well as information about appropriate musical experiences for young children.

Zero to Three

http://www.zerotothree.org

Provides information for professionals, parents, and policy makers on what babies and toddlers need for healthy development.

APPENDIX D:
WISH LISTS FOR FAMILIES

Dear Families,

Don't throw it away! Please save these items and put them in our recycle box. We will use them in dramatic play or creative art and music projects. You will find labeled collection bins next to the door for your donations. Thank you!

Beads

Berry baskets

Bottle caps and tops

Boxes

Bubble wrap

Ceramic tile pieces

Cereal boxes

Cloth shopping bags

Coffee cans

Corks

Costume jewelry

Detergent bottles

Egg cartons

Empty paper-towel rolls

Fabric scraps

Film canisters

Frozen-juice cans

Outgrown children's shoes and boots

Paper or plastic cups

Paper plates

Pie tins

Pinecones

Plastic kitchen utensils

Plastic milk jugs

Pop tops from soft-drink cans

Ribbon

Scarves

Seedpods

Sewing notions

Sheets

Shoe boxes

Small smooth rocks

Socks

Spice cans

Frozen meal trays

Jigsaw puzzles with missing pieces

Juice boxes

Milk cartons

Mismatched nuts, bolts, and washers

Oatmeal boxes

Old keys

Old kitchen utensils

Old wallets and purses

Sponges

Stickers and stamps from junk mail

Styrofoam trays

Tin cans

Wallpaper books and paint samples

Wire hangers

Wood scraps

Wrapping paper

Yarn

DON'T THROW IT AWAY!

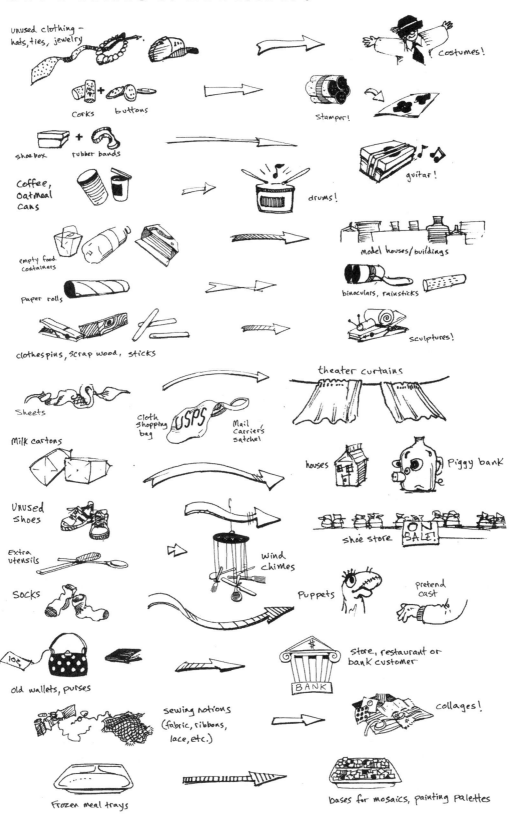

unused clothing — hats, ties, jewelry → costumes!

corks + buttons → stamper!

shoebox + rubber bands → guitar!

Coffee, Oatmeal Cans → drums!

empty food containers → model houses/buildings

paper rolls → binoculars, rainsticks

clothespins, scrap wood, sticks → sculptures!

sheets / cloth shopping bag USPS / Mail Carrier's Satchel → theater curtains

milk cartons → houses / Piggy bank

unused shoes → shoe store ON SALE!

extra utensils → wind chimes

socks → puppets / pretend cast

old wallets, purses → store, restaurant or bank customer / BANK

sewing notions (fabric, ribbons, lace, etc.) → collages!

frozen meal trays → bases for mosaics, painting palettes

REFERENCES

Bronson, Po, and Ashley Merryman. 2010. "The Creativity Crisis." *Newsweek*. July 10. http://www.newsweek.com/creativity-crisis-74665

Campaign for a Commercial-Free Childhood. 2014. *Selected Research on Screen Time and Children.* http://www.commercialfreechildhood.org/resource/children-and-screen-time

Ginsburg, Kenneth. 2007. "The Importance of Play in Promoting Healthy Child Development and Maintaining Strong Parent-Child Bonds." *Pediatrics* 119(1): 182–91. http://pediatrics.aappublications.org/content/119/1/182.full

Illinois State Board of Education. 2013. *Illinois Early Learning and Development Standards.* Springfield, IL: Illinois State Board of Education. http://illinoisearlylearning.org/ields/matter/preface.htm

Moffitt, Terrie, et al. 2011. "A Gradient of Childhood Self-Control Predicts Health, Wealth, and Public Safety." *Proceedings of the National Academy of Sciences of the United States of America* 108(7): 2693–2698. http://www.pnas.org/content/108/7/2693.full

Robinson, Ken. 2006. "Do Schools Kill Creativity?" *TED Talk* transcript. http://www.ted.com/talks/ken_robinson_says_schools_kill_creativity/transcript?language=en

INDEX

A

B

C

F

families, involving, 92–95, 227–229
Fishing, 127–130
Froebel, F., 1

G

gender differences, 13
Ginsburg, K., 2
"Gradient of Childhood Self-Control Predicts Health, Wealth, and Public Safety, A" (Moffitt), 21
Grocery Store, 130–134

H

Hair Salon/Barber Shop, 134–137
Head Start Learning and Development Framework, 31
Heraclitus, 14
Hospital, 138–142

I

IBM, 2, 15
Illinois Early Learning and Development Standards (Katz), 31–32
"Importance of Play in Promoting Healthy Child Development and Maintaining Strong Parent-Child Bonds, The" (Ginsburg), 2

K

Katz, L., 31–32

L

language and literacy development, 26–29
Library, 142–145

M

Malaguzzi, L., 1
media, influence of, 13